PREDICTING YOUR FUTURE
THROUGH ASTROLOGY

PREDICTING YOUR FUTURE THROUGH ASTROLOGY

Sita Ram Singh
M.A., LL.M.
Jyotirvid

Sterling Paperbacks

STERLING PAPERBACKS
An imprint of
Sterling Publishers (P) Ltd.
A-59, Okhla Industrial Area, Phase-II, New Delhi-110020.
Tel: 26387070, 26386209; Fax: 91-11-26383788
E-mail: mail@sterlingpublishers.com
www.sterlingpublishers.com

Predicting Your Future through Astrology
© 2011, Sita Ram Singh
ISBN 978 81 207 5693 9

All rights are reserved.
No part of this publication may be reproduced, stored in a retrieval system or transmitted, in any form or by any means, mechanical, photocopying, recording or otherwise, without prior written permission of the author.

Printed in India

Printed and Published by Sterling Publishers Pvt. Ltd., New Delhi-110 020.

Preface

Indian Astrology is an ancient Divine Science. It was first revealed by *Lord Brahma* to *Surya Dev*, who then taught it to *Trikaldarshi* (omniscient) *Maharishis*. Their disciples recorded the details in Sanskrit language, then common parlance, for the benefit of posterity.

During the long intervening period and foreign invasions some portions of the original treatises were damaged or mutilated which is evident from the variance found in the texts brought out by different publishers. The intricacy of Sanskrit language also caused some variance during translation from Sanskrit to other languages.

The author initially faced some difficulty while learning the subject, as different authors highlighted different aspects in their books. After sifting the fundamental rules, the author first tested these in the horoscope of himself and near and dear ones whose life events were known to him. On gaining confidence he applied these rules in a large number of cases and achieved proficiency. During the last seven years, the author has also contributed to nearly ninety articles on different facets of human life, both in English and Hindi, in leading astrological magazines, like *The Astrological Magazine*, and *Modern Astrology* published from Bangalore; *Star Teller* from Chennai; *Times of Astrology* (English and Hindi), and *BABAJI* (English and Hindi) published from New Delhi. Thus the author has been deeply associated with astrology for over 12 years.

The book comprises 14 Chapters. As correct and detailed horoscopes can now be easily prepared on computer, the author has straightaway started with the elaboration of the basic concepts.

The contents of the book have been presented in a lucid manner so as to maintain interest and inquisitiveness. The Chapters (1)

Rationale of Exaltation of Planets, (2) *Varga* Charts, (3) *Shadabala,* and (4) Retrograde Planets are important as their contents are not available in any book in such detail. The Chapters (1) Inter-relationship of Signs, *Bhava* and Planets, (2) Lucky Births, and (3) Horoscopic Evaluation at First Glance, demonstrate practical application of the rules stated in the book. Liberal use of example horoscopes has been made to facilitate assimilation of the subject.

The author most respectfully dedicates the book to his preceptor and mentor late Shri O.P. Sharma, M.A., former DIG Police, and a profound astrologer, and his wife late Smt. Manju Sharma, M.A., who continue to inspire the author through their benign blessings.

The author is grateful to Mr. Udyan Sharma and his wife Mrs. Ritu Sharma, and his own daughter Mrs. Renu Singh, who have been constantly prompting for early completion of the book.

The author also expresses his sincere thanks to the publisher for bringing out the book in decent form in the shortest possible time.

The author hopes that this humble attempt based on serious study and practice of Astrology for over 12 years will prove a handy compendium to those interested in learning astrology, and will also get the approbation of learned scholars of this Divine Science. Any suggestions for improvement are welcome.

January 1, 2011 **Sita Ram Singh**
8-c DDA Flats Complex, M.A., LL.M
Sarai Juliana, *Jyotirvid*
New Delhi-110025 (India)
Ph: 91-11-26910303
E-mail:astro.srsingh@gmail.com

Contents

	Preface	v
1.	Horoscope	1
2.	Planets	12
3.	Rationale of Exaltation of Planets	19
4.	*Lagna* and *Bhava* Charts	36
5.	Inter-relationship of Sign, *Bhava* and Planets	49
6.	*Nakshatras*	59
7.	*Varga* Charts	69
8.	*Shadabala* of Planets	80
9.	Retrograde Planets	88
10.	Important Planetary Yogas	100
11.	Timing of Events	146
12.	Lucky Births	171
13.	Horoscopic Evaluation at First Glance	184
14.	Epilogue	198

Chapter I

The Horoscope

The Indian Astrology is a Divine Science. It is called वेद चक्षु: (the eyes of *Vedas*). The 12 *Rasis* (signs), 9 *Grahas* (planets), and 27 *Nakshatras* (Constellations) are its basic components. The 12 *Rasis* of 30° each and 27 *Nakshatras* of 13°20' each start from 0° of the zodiac and simultaneously end at 360°. A *Rasi* contains 2¼ *Nakshatra*.

Horoscope is the planetary chart erected for the date, time and place of birth of any individual. The duration of a sign is approximately two hours, and the 12 signs *(Rasis)* rise one after another during 24 hours. The sign rising in the Eastern Horizon at birth is called the First House or *Lagna,* and other signs follow in the fixed order. After evaluating the nature, location, inter-relationship, strength, and *Dasa-Bhukti* of planets, an astrologer foretells the future events in an individual's life.

The horoscope is cast differently in North, South and East India. Treating Leo sign as *Lagna,* the chart in different format will be as under.

	6 Virgo (150°-180°)		4 Cancer (90°-120°)	
7 Libra (180°-210°)		5 Leo (120°-150°)		3 Gemini (60°-90°)
	8 Scorpio (210°-240°)		2 Taurus (30°-60°)	
9 Sagittarius (240°-270°)		11 Aquarius (300°-330°)		1 Aries (0°-30°)
	10 Capricorn (270°-300°)		12 Pisces (330°-360°)	

This chart is used in North India and in some other States as well. Here *Lagna* is indicated in the topmost square and other signs follow serially anti-clockwise. Then planets are posited in different signs according to their position indicated in the Ephemeries (*Panchang*).

Pisces (330°-360°)	Aries (0°-30°)	Taurus (30°-60°)	Gemini (60°-90°)
Aquarius (300°-330°)			Cancer (90°-120°)
Capricorn (270°-300°)			*Lagna* Leo (120°-150°)
Sagittarius (240°-270°)	Scorpio (210°-240°)	Libra (180°-210°)	Virgo (150°-180°)

This chart is primarily used in South India. The signs are fixed and move clockwise. The location of *Lagna* is written in the sign it falls, and planetary position indicated.

Taurus (30°-60°)	Aries (0°-30°)		Pisces (330°-360°)
Gemini (60°-90°)			Aquarius (300°-330°)
Cancer (90°-120°)			Capricorn (270°-300°)
Lagna Leo (120°-150°)	Libra (180°-210°)		Sagittarius (240°-270°)
Virgo (150°-180°)			Scorpio (210°-240°)

This chart is used in East India. Here also the signs are fixed. These move towards left. *Lagna* is indicated in the sign it falls and planetary position indicated.

The planets, except Rahu and Ketu, have forward motion, unless they become retrograde occasionally. On the contrary, Rahu and Ketu always move in reverse direction, i.e. from 5th to 4th, 3rd and so on.

The example horoscopes have been displayed both in North India and South India formats.

The *Rasis*

The fixed Zodiac of 360° has been divided in 12 equal signs (*Rasis*) of 30° each. Starting from 0° of the Zodiac, these signs are *in seriatim* named as Aries, Taurus, Gemini, Cancer, Leo, Virgo, Libra, Scorpio, Sagittarius, Capricorn, Aquarius and Pisces. The 12 signs are allotted to different planets according to their mutual compatability. The Sun and the Moon are allotted one sign each, Leo and Cancer respectively. Mars is lord of Aries and Scorpio. Venus is lord of Taurus and Libra. Mercury rules over Gemini and Virgo. Jupiter rules over Sagittarius and Pisces, and Saturn rules over Capricorn and Aquarius. Rahu and Ketu, being *Chhayagrahas* (without matter) are not allotted any sign.

As regards their nature, Aries, Cancer, Libra and Capricorn are Movable; Taurus, Leo, Scorpio and Aquarius are Fixed; and Gemini, Virgo, Sagittarius and Pisces are Common (or dual) signs. Further, Aries, Gemini, Leo, Libra, Sagittarius and Aquarius are odd, male and positive signs; and the remaining signs are even, female and negative in nature. Besides, Aries, Leo, Sagittarius are Fiery in nature; Taurus, Virgo and Capricorn are Earthy; Gemini, Libra and Aquarius are Airy signs; while Cancer, Scorpio and Pisces are Watery signs. These characteristics influence the *Bhava* (house) and planets located therein.

The 12 signs rule over the body organs as follows. Aries-head; Taurus-face, neck; Gemini-shoulders, arms and upper chest; Cancer-breast and heart; Leo-stomach, spine and back; Virgo-intestines and waist; Libra-area below navel and internal sex organs; Scorpio-urinary and outer genitals; Sagittarius-hips and thighs; Capricorn-knees; Aquarius-calves and ankles; and Pisces-soles and toes. Malefics in any sign of the horoscope cause weakness or disease of concerned body part.

Depending on the time and place of birth, any of the 12 signs can occupy *Lagna*. Each *Rasi* rises in *Lagna* for approximately two hours. The Sun occupies the *Lagna* at sunrise, the 10th house at noon, the 7th house at sunset, and the 4th house at midnight. *Lagna* is strong when Gemini, Virgo, Libra, first half of Sagittarius or Aquarius is located there. Scorpio *Lagna* is only one-fourth strong, and the remaining signs in *Lagna* are of medium strength. Leo, Virgo, Libra, Scorpio and Aquarius are strong in *Lagna* during day birth, while Aries, Taurus, Gemini, Cancer, Sagittarius and Capricon are strong during night birth. Pisces is strong both during day and night birth.

Rasi occupied by a planet is stronger than the *Rasi* having no planet in it. A *Rasi* having more number of planets is considered stronger than that having lesser number of planets. In case of equal number of planets, the *Rasi* having an exalted planet, or one in *Mooltrikona* or in own sign is considered stronger. Finally, movable, fixed and common *Rasis* are progressively stronger.

When the *Lagna* and its lord are strong by location, conjunction or aspect of benefic planets without malefic influence, it ensures a comfortable life to the individual. The *Lagna Nakshatra* Lord (LNL) and the lord of Moon *Nakshatra* lord strongly placed in an auspicious house confirm good result.

The *Bhavas*

Counted *seriatim* from *Lagna* onwards the *Rasis* (signs) acquire the name of *Bhava* (house), which represent different facets of human life from birth to death, namely, self (birth), wealth, siblings, mother, progeny, enemy, wife, longevity, luck, profession, gains and loss (death). These are also called 1st, 2nd, 3rd .... 12th houses respectively. The 1st to 6th houses represent the right side limbs of the individual and 7th to 12th houses represent the left side limbs.

Among the 12 houses, 1st, 4th, 7th and 10th houses are called *Kendras,* and 1st, 5th and 9th houses are called *Trikonas*. *Lagna* is both a *Kendra* and *Trikona* and becomes important. Planets are strong in *Kendra* and *Trikona*. These have medium strength in *Panphar* (2, 5, 8 and 11th - next to *Kendra*) houses, and are least powerful in *Apoklim* (3, 6, 9 and 12th - prior to *Kendra*) houses. The *Trines* are auspicious houses, and when occupied by benefics these become most auspicious, and their lords give good result in their *Dasa-Bhukti*. The 3rd, 6th, 10th and 11th houses are called *Upachaya* (growth). However, the planets owning 3rd, 6th and 11th houses do not give good result during their *Dasa-Bhukti*.

The 6th, 8th and 12th houses are called *Trika* or *Duststhana* (evil houses) among which the 8th house is considered the most evil. When the lord of any house is posited in *Trika* (evil) house or an evil house lord occupies any other house, then that house matters suffer. But when an evil house lord is posited in any evil house, and also afflicted it gives good result. This is called *Vipreet Rajyoga* (negative + negative = positive).

The 8th house refers to longevity and also nature and place of death. *Lagna* lord, the Sun and Moon are free from blemish of 8th house lordship. According to the principle of *Bhavat Bhavam,* the 3rd house (8th to 8th) is also regarded house of longevity. The 12th house (loss) from 8th and 3rd house, i.e., 7th and 2nd house are called *marak* (loss of longevity) house, and their lords are called *marakas* (dangerous to longevity). Jupiter and Venus, if lord of 7th and 2nd house, and posited therein become strong *Maraka*. When Saturn becomes associated with 7th or 2nd house lord, then it takes over *marak* function itself, and becomes first rate *Maraka*.

Significations of 12 Houses

The main significations (*Karkatwa*) of different houses are as follows:

1st House (*Lagna*) : Refers to body and head in particular. It indicates one's health, complexion, nature, status and prosperity in life.

2nd House: Refers to wealth, family, basic education, speech, expression, face, nose, mouth, right eye and eating habits.

3rd House: Refers to younger siblings, courage, valour, perseverance, enterprise, throat, right ear, right arm, shoulders, upper chest, writing and communication.

4th House: Refers to mother, mentality, education, house, relatives, happiness, scents, conveyance, cattle wealth, property, land and agricultural fields, chest, heart, jewellery, dress material and garments.

5th House: Refers to love, affection, progeny, wit, wisdom, stomach, education, poetic skill, foresight, ministerial rank, *Mantra Jap* and *Siddhi*.

6th House: Refers to enemy, debt, theft, wound, boils, disease, worry, obstacles, fear, humiliation, litigation, competition, maternal uncle, waist, lower stomach, colic, urinary and eye disease.

7th House: Refers to marriage, partnership, business, spouse, sex, internal sex organs and their diseases.

8th House: Refers to longevity, cause of death, hidden wealth, speculation, gambling, secret knowledge, research, *Mangalya* (happiness of married life), external genitals, worry, defeat, insult, evil deeds, annoying situations, scandal, obstacles and death.

9th House: Refers to *Bhagya* (luck), father, *Acharya* (preceptor) deity, travel, religion, worship, *Tapas* (austerity), virtuous deeds, thighs and grandson.

10th House: Refers to profession, trade, status, honour, fame, respect, success, conduct, reputation, bent of mind, command, authority and knees.

11th House: Refers to gains, income, acquisition, fulfilment of desires, wealth, ornaments, profit, praise, elder brother, left ear, left hand, calves and happy news.

12th House: Refers to loss, misery, lower leg, left eye, secret inimical activity, poverty, sin, bed comforts, sleep, nature of expenditure, imprisonment, hospitalisation and end of life.

IMPORTANT GUIDELINES

When the lord of any house is in *Kendra* or *Trikona* from *Lagna* or Moon, is in its own sign, *Mooltrikona* or exaltation sign, and aspected by unafflicted benefics (Jupiter, Venus and Mercury) that individual enjoys the matters of that house.

A planet in the middle of a sign (12° to 18°) gives maximum result of the house and the least in the first 6° and the last 6° of the sign. It gives middling result between 6° to 12°, and 18° to 24°. A benefic or a malefic planet occupying or aspecting its own sign augments the result of that house.

When the dispositor of a planet (i.e., the lord of the house where a planet is posited) is strong by location, conjunction or aspect of benefics, the house under consideration and the planet therein gain in strength, and give good result. If the dispositor is weak or ill-posited or afflicted, the matters of the house under consideration suffer.

Benefic planets on both sides of a house strengthen the house and improve that house matters. It is called *Shubha Kartari Yoga*, while malefics on both sides of a house form *Pap Kartari Yoga* and weaken that house matters.

When lord of any house goes to 6th, 8th or 12th house or to inimical sign or becomes *Asta* (combust by the Sun), then the planets posited in that house become incapable of augmenting that house matters.

Lagna lord associated with any house or its lord will give full result of that house provided that house lord is strong.

When any house is occupied or aspected by its lord or benefics, without any evil influence, that house matters prosper.

A malefic planet in own sign or friendly sign or *Navamsa* also improves the matters of that house, by virtue of being comfortable. But if that malefic planet is posited in its debilitation or an inimical sign/*Navamsa* or conjoined with malefic planet then it harms that house matters.

When planets in 2nd, 3rd or 11th from any house are friendly to that house lord then these planets increase the matters of the house under consideration.

If from the house under consideration the 6th, 8th and 12th house are occupied by malefics, then benefics located in the house under consideration become ineffective to augment that house matters.

If benefics are posited in 2nd, 12th, 4th, 8th and *Trikona* (5th and 9th) houses from any house, then that house prospers. But malefics in these places spoil that house matters. The debility of a house lord also destroys that house matters.

Benefics as lord of *Kendra* do not give good result, while malefics as lord of *Kendra* do not give bad result. Lords of 5th and 9th houses, whether benefic or malefic, always give good result.

When the 11th house (gains) lord is placed in any house, or the 11th lord is conjoined with the lord of any house, then that house matters prosper. For example, if the 11th lord is in 2nd house, then it will give gain of wealth. If 11th lord is with 5th lord, then the native has good education and happiness from progeny.

Benefics in the 3rd, 6th and 11th *(Upachaya)* houses give happiness in childhood, while malefics therein make old age happy.

When there are benefics in *Kendra* or *Trikona* from a house under consideration, and these are also lords of good house, without any evil effect, that house matters prosper.

A house occupied by a planet is stronger than the one which is vacant. A house with greater number of planets is stronger than the one with lesser number of planets. In the event of equal occupancy, the house with stronger planets is considered stronger. If uncertainty persists then the house with a Movable, Fixed or Common sign is progressively stronger.

When *Lagna*, 2nd, 7th, 9th and 11th houses are strong and occupied by benefic planets, the native leads a happy and prosperous life.

When any house lord and that house *Karka* (significator) are exalted but occupy *Trika* (6, 8 or 12) house, the native does not get the result of that house. On the contrary, if the house lord and its *Karka* are in inimical sign or debilitated but posited in good house, then the native gets some result of that house.

The result of any house is experienced commensurate with the strength of its lord, during operation of its *Dasa-Bhukti*, when it is also strong during transit. When the lord of that house and *Lagna* lord are conjoined or in *Trine* to that house, or to each other in transit, the house result fructify. That house lord's transit through *Lagna* is also fruitful.

Natural benefics in *Kendra* from the *Lagna* or *Lagna* lord make the horoscope strong.

An individual with ordinary horoscope born in rich family leads a comfortable life, while an individual born in a poor family with strong planetary *Yogas* will gradually rise in life. The *Dasas* of favourable planets to the horoscope should also operate in youth to provide a solid base to the individual's life.

RECAPITULATION

Nature of *Rasis* (signs)

Fiery	-	Aries, Leo and Sagittarius.
Earthy	-	Taurus, Virgo and Capricorn.
Airy	-	Gemini, Libra and Aquarius.
Watery	-	Cancer, Scorpio and Pisces.
Movable	-	Aries, Cancer, Libra and Capricorn.
Fixed	-	Taurus, Leo, Scorpio and Aquarius.
Common	-	Gemini, Virgo, Sagittarius and Pisces.
Positive (male) (odd)	-	Aries, Gemini, Leo, Libra, Sagittarius and Aquarius.
Negative (female) (even)	-	Taurus, Cancer, Virgo, Scorpio, Capricorn and Pisces.

Body parts ruled by Signs

Aries	-	Head.
Taurus	-	Face.
Gemini	-	Throat, shoulders and upper chest.
Cancer	-	Breast, lungs and heart.
Leo	-	Stomach, spine and back.
Virgo	-	Intestines and waist region.
Libra	-	Internal private parts, area below navel.
Scorpio	-	Urinary and external private parts.
Sagittarius	-	Hips and thighs.
Capricorn	-	Knees.
Aquarius	-	Calves and ankles.
Pisces	-	Soles, toes.

The Horoscope

Planets	Signs ruled
Sun	Leo.
Moon	Cancer.
Mercury -	Gemini and Virgo.
Venus -	Taurus and Libra.
Mars -	Aries and Scorpio.
Jupiter -	Sagittarius and Pisces.
Saturn -	Capricorn and Aquarius.
Rahu/Ketu -	No sign allotted.

Houses	
Kendras -	1, 4, 7, 10.
Trikona -	1, 5, 9.
Panphara -	2, 5, 8, 11.
Apoklim -	3, 6, 9, 12.
Trika -	6, 8, 12.
Upchaya -	3, 6, 10, 11.

A Sign (*Rasi*) comprises 30° (degrees). A degree (°) has 60 minutes (') and a minute has 60 seconds ("). A planet's position in a sign is indicated as ° ' " (e.g., 5° 25' 30").

Chapter II
Planets

Out of the numerous planets in *Brahamand* (space) our visionary *Rishis* had selected 9 planets for divining future. Among these nine planets Jupiter, Venus, *Pakshabali* Moon and unafflicted Mercury are benefics. The Sun is regarded cruel. Saturn, Mars, Rahu and Ketu are malefic. Though, Rahu and Ketu are without matter (only mathematical points), because of their profound influence on human beings these have been accorded the status of planet.

The Sun

The Sun is the king of our solar system. It signifies *Atma* (soul), father, gold, courage, power, success, Government service, right eye, *Yajna*, temple, mental sharpness, initiative, drive and authoritative position. It rules East direction. Its colour is golden-red and gem *Manik* (Ruby). Jupiter, Mars and Moon are its friends. Mercury is Sun's neutral; while Saturn, Venus, Rahu and Ketu are its enemies. Sun rules over Leo sign, is exalted in Aries (upto 10°) and debilitated in opposite sign Libra. Its *Mooltrikona* sign is Leo upto 20° and the rest is own sign.

The Moon

The Moon is the Queen of the solar system and rules North-West direction. It signifies mother, mind, sea related items, white colour, fruits, flowers, liquids, silky attire, soft cushions, agriculture, reputation, silver, cows, milk, sweets, food delicacies, physical charm and left eye. Its gem is *Moti* (white Pearl). The Sun and Mercury are its friends, Rahu enemy, and the rest are neutral. It owns Cancer, sign. It is exalted in Taurus sign (upto 3°) and debilitated in opposite sign Scorpio. Its *Mooltrikona* sign is Taurus (after 3°). A *Pakashabali* Moon confers wealth during its *Dasa* and *Bhukti* when aspected by a planet in exaltation or in own sign.

Mars

Mars is the Commander-in-Chief of our solar system, and it rules South direction. It signifies physical strength, prowess and bravery, all that grows on earth, youth, younger siblings, cruelty, courage, enemity, kitchen, fire, weapons, thieves, enemies, red colour, adultery, falsehood, wickedness, wound, injury, and service in Police or Army. Its gem is *Moonga* (red Coral). The Sun, Moon and Jupiter are its friends; Saturn, Rahu and Mercury are enemy, and Venus is neutral. Mars is exalted in Capricorn (28°) and debilitated in its opposite sign Cancer. Its *Mooltrikona* sign is Aries (upto 12°), the remaining portion and Scorpio its own sign.

Mercury

Mercury is regarded the prince (*Kumar*) of the solar system and rules North direction. It refers to speech, learning, truthfulness, eloquence, fine arts, skills, maternal uncle, *Yajna*, devotion to Lord Vishnu, proficiency in craft, relatives, friends, and application of intelligence in learning. Its gem is *Panna* (Emerald), and colour green. Venus, Rahu and the Sun are Mercury's friends; Moon is enemy; and Jupiter, Saturn and Mars are neutrals. It owns Gemini and Virgo signs. It is exalted in Virgo upto 15° and debilitated in opposite sign Pisces. Its *Mooltrikona* is Virgo 15° to 20°, and the rest portion is its own sign. It is never more than 28° away from the Sun.

Jupiter

Jupiter is the Minister of solar cabinet and rules North-East direction. It denotes knowledge, learning, noble qualities, good behaviour, son, teaching profession, magnanimity, knowledge of *Vedas*, reverence to God, *Yajna*, worship, religious faith, wisdom, wealth, control over passions, honour and compassion. In female chart it shows husband's happiness (*Mangalya*). It is significator for son, and the elder brother, its colour is yellow and gem is *Pukhraj* (yellow Sapphire). The Sun, Mars and Moon are its friends; Venus, Mercury and Rahu are enemy; and Saturn neutral. It is exalted in Cancer sign (5°) and debilitated at 5° in opposite sign Capricorn. Its *Mooltrikona* sign is Sagittarius upto 10°, the remaining portion and Pisces own sign.

Venus

Venus is also the Minister of solar Cabinet, and rules South-East direction. It signifies luxury, sex, wealth, vehicles, fine clothes, ornaments, hidden wealth, dance, drama, poetry, music, wife, conjugal bliss, scents, flowers, excellent house, prosperity, fair sex, lustfulness, politeness, marriage and festivities. In male horoscope it is significator for wife and conjugal happiness. Its gem is *Hira* (Diamond). Saturn, Rahu and Mercury are its friends; Jupiter and Mars are neutral, and the Sun and Moon are its enemies. It rules Taurus and Libra sign. It is exalted in Pisces (27°) and is debilitated in opposite sign Virgo (27°). Its *Mooltrikona* sign is Libra (0° to 15°) and the rest is its own sign. It is never more than 48° away from the Sun.

Saturn

Saturn signifies lower class of society and hardship in life. It relates to longevity, death, fear, defamation, misery, difficulties, sickness, poverty, laborious menial work, sin, impurity, misfortune, buffalo, lethargy, debt, servitude, agricultural tool, litigation and captivity. Saturn gives stability to the house where it is posited, but it harms the house aspected by it. Its gem is blue Sapphire (*Neelam*). It rules West direction. Venus, Rahu and Mercury are its friends; Jupiter is neutral to Saturn, and the Sun, Moon and Mars are its enemies. It owns Capricorn and Aquarius signs of the Zodiac. It is exalted in Libra (20°) and is debilitated in opposite sign Aries. Aquarius is its *Mooltrikona* sign (0° to 20°) and the rest its own sign.

Rahu

Rahu denotes outcaste and darkness. It rules South-West direction. Rahu represents low caste, skin ailments, leprosy, falsehood, cunningness, speaking ill of others, shrewed intellect, poison and fear of snake bite. Lead and rags belong to Rahu. Saturn, Venus and Mercury are friends of Rahu, and the Sun, Moon, Mars and Jupiter are inimical. Rahu's conjunction with Mars forms malefic *Angarak* (Fiery) *Yoga,* and with Jupiter *Guru-Chandal Yoga*. Its colour is black and gem is Hessonite (*Gomed*). With difference of opinion, Rahu is exalted in Taurus/Gemini, and debilitated in Scorpio/Sagittarius.

Ketu

Ketu relates to outcaste, smoking, cruelty, loss through theft, injury marks on body, bitter speech and back-biting. Clay utensils and multi-coloured clothes come under the domain of Ketu. Its exaltation and debilitation signs are opposed to Rahu. It is effiminate. Its colour is smoky and its gem is Cat's Eye (*Lahsuniya*). Mercury, Venus, Saturn are friends, Mars is neutral, and Sun, Moon and Jupiter are enemies.

IMPORTANT GUIDELINES

1. Jupiter is the most powerful among benefic planets. Venus has half benefic power than Jupiter, and Mercury has one-fourth power than Jupiter. Moon and Mercury with Jupiter and Venus give good result. Benefics are strong in bright fortnight (*Shukla Paksha*).

2. Moon's strength lies in its *Pakshabal* (being more than 72° away from the Sun). Moon has maximum strength at *Purnima* (full moon day). Strong Moon removes many defects or shortcomings in the horoscope. The sign occupied by the Moon is also treated as *Lagna*.

3. The waning (decreasing in light) Moon, Mars, Rahu, Ketu and Saturn are malefic planets. Mercury in association with malefics becomes malefic. Malefics are strong in dark fortnight (*Krishna Paksha*).

4. The Sun is regarded cruel. It is strong during day birth, in the 10th house of the horoscope, and in *Uttarayan* (transit from Capricorn to Gemini).

5. The Sun, Mars and Jupiter are male planets. Venus, Rahu and Moon are female, while Ketu, Mercury and Saturn are enunch.

6. The planets give their result as follows – in friendly sign 25%, own sign 50%, *Mooltrikona* 75% and in exaltation 100%. When a planet occupies the same sign in *Lagna* Chart and *Navamsa* Chart, it becomes *Vargottam* and gives result like in *Mooltrikona* (75%).

7. When the planets are strong and well placed in the horoscope, these give favourable result in their specific year as under:–

Jupiter	— 16th year	The Sun	— 22nd year
The Moon	— 24th year	Venus	— 25th year
Mars	— 28th year	Mercury	— 32nd year
Saturn	— 36th year	Rahu and Ketu	— 42nd year

8. When a planet becomes lord of a *Kendra* and *Trikona* house in the horoscope, it becomes *Yogakarka* (very favourable) – like Mars for Cancer and Leo *Lagna*; Saturn for Taurus and Libra *Lagna*, and Venus for Capricorn and Aquarius *Lagna*. But if the *Yogakarka* is afflicted by malefics or posited in 6th, 8th or 12th, its capability to give benefic result gets reduced.

9. An exalted or strong planet aspected by malefics does not give expected result, while a debilitated or ill-posited planet aspected by benefics does not do much harm by virtue of its bad location or malefic effect.

10. When the planets are combust by Sun, debilitated, in inimical sign, or in 6th, 8th or 12th houses from *Lagna*, or at the last degree of *Rasi* (sign), (except in dual Signs, where it gets *Vargottam*) these are considered ill-posited, and become incapable of giving good result of the house owned and where located.

11. Planets become functional (temporary) friends if these occupy the 2nd, 3rd, 4th, 10th, 11th and 12th houses from one another. Functional friends and natural friends become *Adhimitra* (best friend). Natural as well as functional enemy planets become *Adhishatru* (bitter enemies).

12. When a planet is lord of one benefic and another malefic house and if it is strong it will give result of good house, and if weak then of malefic house.

13. A planet gives primarily the result of its *Mooltrikona* sign, and much lesser of the house where its other sign falls.

14. All the planets aspect the 7th house (opposite to their location). The following planets have special full aspect in addition to 7th. The aspect of a planet is more powerful than its occupation of a house.

    Jupiter — 5th and 9th   Mars — 4th and 8th
    Saturn — 3rd and 10th   Rahu/Ketu — 5th and 9th
    (Some authorities differ as these are only mathematical points).

15. A person enjoys the result of any house in full when that house, its lord, and *Karka* planets are strong by association and aspect of benefic planets. The *Karka* for different houses are as under:

    1st House — Sun
    2nd House — Jupiter
    3rd House — Mars
    4th House — Moon and Mercury
    5th House — Jupiter
    6th House — Saturn and Mars
    7th House — Venus
    8th House — Saturn
    9th House — Sun and Jupiter.
    10th House — Sun, Jupiter, Saturn and Mercury
    11th House — Jupiter
    12th House — Saturn

    Thus Jupiter is *Karka* for 5 houses and Saturn for 4 houses.

16. When a *Karka* is posited in the house of which it is *Karka*, it does not give good result of that house as per the *dicta* 'कारको भाव नाशाय'. The reason is that if it becomes afflicted then two factors – the House and *Karka* are spoilt.

17. When Jupiter is not lord of evil house and well-posited in the horoscope, the individual leads a prosperous life.

18. When Saturn is ill-posited or afflicted, the individual suffers in his life.

The final assessment should be made after complete analysis of the horoscope, social status of the individual and sequence of *Dasas*.

Recapitulation

Planet	Nature	Friend	Neutral	Enemy	Exaltation	Debilitation
1. The Sun	Hot, dry, male, *Kshatriya*	Moon, Mars, Jupiter	Mercury	Saturn, Venus, Rahu, Ketu.	Aries (1°-10°)	Libra (1°-10°)
2. The Moon	Cold, moist, female, *Vaishya*.	Sun, Mercury	All other planets	None	Taurus (1°-3°)	Scorpio (1°-3°)
3. Mars	Hot, dry, male, *kshatriya*	Sun, Moon, Jupiter	Venus	Saturn, Rahu, Mercury	Capricorn (1°-28°)	Cancer (1°-28°)
4. Mercury	Cold, dry, Neuter, *Vaishya*	Sun Venus	Moon	Mars, Jupiter, Saturn	Virgo (1°-15°)	Pisces (1°-15°)
5. Jupiter	Hot, dry, male, *Brahmin*	Sun, Moon, Mars	Saturn	Mercury, Venus, Rahu	Cancer (1°-5°)	Capricorn (1°-5°)
6. Venus	Moist, female, *Brahmin*	Mercury, Saturn	Jupiter Mars	Sun, Moon	Pisces (1°-27°)	Virgo (1°-27°)
7. Saturn	Cold, dry, Neuter, *Shudra*	Venus, Mercury	Jupiter	Sun, Mars, Moon	Libra (1°-20°)	Aries (1°-20°)
8. Rahu	Like Saturn	Saturn, Venus, Mercury		Sun, Moon, Mars, Jupiter	Taurus (Gemini)	Scorpio (Sagittarius)
9. Ketu	Like Mars.	Mercury, Venus	Mars	Sun, Moon Jupiter	Scorpio (Sagittarius)	Taurus (Gemini)

Chapter III
Rationale of Exaltation of Planets

The quality and quantity of the results produced by the nine planets depends on their strength, whether in exaltation, *Mooltrikona*, own, friendly or enemy sign, and whether in a benefic or malefic house. According to *Phaladeepika*:

तुङ्गस्था बलिनोऽखिलाश्च शशिन: शलाध्यं हि पक्षोद्भवं ।
भानोर्दिग्बलमाह बक्रगमने ताराग्रहाणां बलम् ।

(Ch. 4.5)

meaning, "All planets are strong when they occupy their exaltation sign. The Moon is strong and auspicious when it has *Pakshabala,* and the Sun has *Digbala* in 10th house. The remaining planets are strong when they are in their retrograde motion." Rahu and Ketu are always in retrograde motion.

Phaladeepika further states:

एकोऽप्युच्चक्षेत्रगो मित्रदृष्ट:
कूर्यादभूपं मित्रयोगाढ्नाढ्यम्।

(Ch. 7.21)

meaning, "Even if there is one single planet posited in its highest exaltation and is aspected by a friendly planet, it makes one King. If such exalted planet is conjoined with another friendly planet, the native become extremely rich."

Our ancient *Rishis* have assigned *Ucchasthan* (exaltation sign) to all the nine planets, and the opposite sign is their *Neechasthan* (debilitation sign). The highest exaltation and debilitation degree in different *Rasis* (signs) are tabulated below:

Planet	Highest Exaltation Sign/Degree	Highest Debilitation Sign/Degree
Sun	Aries 10°	Libra 10°
Moon	Taurus 3°	Scorpio 3°
Mars	Capricorn 28°	Cancer 28°
Mercury	Virgo 15°	Pisces 15°
Venus	Pisces 27°	Virgo 27°
Jupiter	Cancer 5°	Capricorn 5°
Saturn	Libra 20°	Aries 20°
Rahu	Gemini	Sagittarius } Majority
Ketu	Sagittarius	Gemini } view

As regards the quantum of result given by a planet, *Phaladeepika* further states:

स्वोच्चे पूर्णं स्वत्रिकोणे त्रिपदं स्वक्षेत्रर्द्धं पादमेव।
द्विक्षेत्रेऽल्पं नीचगेऽस्तंगतेऽपि क्षेत्रं वीर्यं निष्फलं स्याद् ग्रहाणाम् ॥

(Ch. 4.7)

meaning, "The positional strength of a planet is full (100%) when it is in exaltation. Its strength is ¾ (75%) when in its *Mooltrikona* sign. It has ½ (50%) strength when posited in own sign, and its strength is ¼ (25%) in friend's sign. In an inimical sign, the planet has little strength. Its strength is 'nil' when it is debilitated or eclipsed by the rays of the Sun."

The planets give their result during their *Dasa* and *Bhukti*. When the *Dasa* of an exalted planet operates around youth, it provides a solid platform for rise in life.

While the exaltation of the Sun, Moon, Mercury, Venus and Jupiter improves their benefic qualities, the exaltation of Saturn, Mars, Rahu and Ketu reduces their evil propensities. An exalted planet, however, fails to fulfil the expectations when it is aspected by, or associated with, strong malefic, or is debilitated in *Navamsa* Chart. If the horoscope is inherently weak, the presence of an exalted planet alone may not do much good to the individual.

Rationale of Exaltation of Planets

While highlighting the results produced by exalted planets, the Astrological classics do not elucidate the reasons for assigning this position. Some scholars have hinted about it in brief. These reasons in detail are as follows.

The Sun

The Vedic name of the Sun is '*Aditya*' which means 'of unchangeable nature.' Accordingly, the Sun symbolizes immortal soul. Another name of the Sun is '*Bhaskara*', which means 'the source of light.' Since human eyes are the instruments for seeing light, there is an intimate connection between the Sun and the eyes. Yet another name of the Sun is '*Savitri*' meaning 'the inspirer'. Astrologically, the Sun inspires spirituality (love of God).

Aries, the first sign of the Zodiac, owned by Mars, has been assigned the exaltation sign to Sun. In the natural Zodiac, Aries is the 9th house from Sun's sign Leo. Aries sign is a Male, Fiery, Positive and Movable sign. The Sun is a Fixed luminary with Fiery element. Mars, the owner of Aries, is Sun's friend whose qualities of courage and dynamism go well with the Sun's love of authority and supremacy. Aries is also a Male and Fiery sign which suits Sun's nature. However, the Sun in exaltation gets dazzling light and power, which adversely affects the eyesight of the native and makes him overbearing and pompous.

The highest exaltation degree of the Sun is 10° in Aries, which falls in *Aswini Nakashatra*, whose lord Ketu is significator for '*moksha*'. Aries represents active surroundings. The Sun in *Aswini Nakshatra* inspires spirituality. In spite of active life, the native remains conscious of the goal of his life, i.e., liberation or realization of God.

The Sun is in deep debilitation at 10° in Libra sign owned by Venus, in *Swati Nakshatra* owned by Rahu. Both the sign and *Nakshatra* lords are inimical to the Sun. The Sun is Fiery, whereas Venus is a Watery planet, and Rahu causes *Grahana* (eclipse of the Sun). In such adverse surroundings, the Sun is not able to express its qualities which get toned down. Hence, the Sun is considered debilitated in Libra. Sun in Libra gives poor health, fluctuating career and little happiness from marriage.

The Moon

The Moon is called *'Soma'* in the *Vedas*, which means 'a refreshing drink'. The other name *'Chandra'* means 'the sense of pleasure'. Hence, happiness and pleasure (experienced through mind) and gentle feelings and compassion (found in mother) are astrologically related to the Moon. Any affliction to Moon, the 4th house, and its lord adversely affect individual's peace of mind and his mother's health. Waning Moon in Aries and Scorpio becomes a strong malefic.

While the Sun is the king of the solar system, the Moon is regarded the queen. The Sun represents soul and the Moon symbolizes mind. As the Moon is Queen of the King Sun, the adjacent second sign of the zodiac is assigned to the Moon as its exaltation sign beside the Sun. In the natural Zodiac, Taurus is the 11th house from Cancer owned by the Moon, signifying fulfilment of desires.

The highest exaltation degree of Moon is 3° in Taurus, in *Kritika Nakshatra*, whose lord is the Sun. As already stated the Sun represents *Atma* (soul). The Moon representing the mind is in its best state when in harmony with soul.

Taurus is a Fixed and Earthy sign and controls Moon's flight of imagination and makes the native worldly wise and practical. The tender nature of Moon finds an easy expression in the feminine Venusian sign of Taurus. The Watery nature of the Moon also finds a fertile ground in the Earthy sign Taurus. A strong Ascendant and strong Moon make the individual rich, prosperous and contented. One seldom finds a person with strong Moon in Taurus either poor or unhappy.

The Moon is in deep debilitation at 3° in Scorpio sign, which is Watery, Fixed, and the Negative sign of Mars, a Fiery planet. Water and fire are inimical in nature. In the selfish sign of Scorpio, the sensitivity of Moon is adversely affected. The Martian influence makes Moon reckless and whimsical. The Moon represents 4th house and rules lungs. A weak and afflicted Moon in Scorpio makes the individual susceptible to diseases of lungs like dropsy and T.B., and also indicates a sickly childhood, as Moon governs childhood. An afflicted Moon in the 12th house adversely affects the left eye. Moon in *Neecha Rasi* or *Navamsa* reduces many good features apparent in the horoscope.

Mars

The Vedic name of Mars is '*Angaraka*', meaning 'burning coal'. The name amply denotes the Fiery nature of Mars and its red colour. Red colour represents energy, blood, muscles, ambition, adventure and enterprise. It represents the army, police and workshops. A Martian native acts in haste without thought. An afflicted or ill-placed Mars causes quarrels, accidents, and injury. Its location in *Lagna*, 2nd, 4th, 7th, 8th or 12th houses of a horoscope causes *Mangal Dosha* which adversely affects married life in males and females.

Mars gets highest exaltation at 28° in Capricorn ruled by Saturn, but in own *Nakshatra Dhanishta*. Saturn, the lord of Capricorn sign, is a bitter enemy of Mars. As a true soldier, Mars is at its best in enemy's camp but well-guarded in its own *Nakshatra*, always alert and cautious. It is no more rash and develops a sense of caution and restraint. The Earthy sign of Capricorn also suits Mars who is called *Bhumiputra* (the son of earth). In the sign of cool and calculative Saturn, Mars also acquires the virtue of reflection before action. In the natural zodiac, from Aries (the positive sign of Mars) Capricorn is the 10th house, and Mars gets *Sthanbala* (positional strength) in the 10th house.

Mars gets deeply debilitated at 28° in Cancer, a Watery sign, in *Ashlesha Nakshatra*, ruled by inimical Mercury. Such a setting is detrimental to the nature, energy and enterprise of Mars. In Cancer, the sign of imaginative Moon, and inimical Mercury *Nakshatra*, the Martian characteristic of aggression without reflection gets accentuated into recklessness. It is like applying brake to a vehicle running at full speed which results in loss of control and balance. Hence, Mars is quite uncomfortable in Cancer sign, and is rightly considered debilitated there.

Mercury

The Vedic name of Mercury is '*Buddha*' which means related to *Buddhi* (intellect). Astrology regards Mercury as significator of intellect, education and speech. Because of the relationship of consciousness and knowledge, Mercury is also known as 'the knower'. Mercury, as

Prince of solar system, is young and changeable planet, of dual nature, and owns two dual signs Gemini and Virgo. It is easily influenced by the company of other planets.

Mercury is the second quickest moving planet after the Moon. Because of changeability, Mercury lacks steadiness. In Astrology, Mercury is called *Kumar* (young boy) who needs guidance and support. The Mercurians, like creepers, require a strong support to blossom fully. Mercurians are very good advisers but they seldom succeed independently.

Out of the four dual signs of the Zodiac, the Fiery sign of Sagittarius does not suit Mercurial nature. The Watery and Mystic sign of Pisces is also not congenial to Mercury. Both Sagittarius and Pisces are opposite to Mercury's own signs – Gemini and Virgo. Gemini is Mercury's Positive sign, an intellectual sign, and helps in improving Mercurial imagination. However, Mercury finds a better ground in Earthy and its Negative sign of Virgo, where it becomes practical, pragmatic and strong.

The highest exaltation degree of Mercury is 15° of Virgo, in the *Nakshatra* of *Hasta* owned by Moon. Mercury represents intellect, while Moon represents feelings and imagination. When intellect retains its logic and is considerate to others as well, nothing could be more noble than that. The rationale of Mercury's exaltation in Virgo is, therefore, in consonance with practical, spiritual and psychological angle.

As stated above, Pisces is not congenial to Mercury where it is regarded debilitated. Its deepest debilitation degree is 15° in Saturn's *Nakshatra*. Although it is a common belief that Mercury is enemy of Jupiter, the intuition of Mercury combined with the wisdom of Jupiter produces learned scholars and successful astrologers.

Venus

The Vedic name of Venus is '*Shukra*', which means sensual, seminal and refined. Hence, Venus represents everything that is refined, such as fine arts, ornaments, luxury items, vehicles, conjugal relationship, and all other worldly comforts (*Iha-loka-sukha*). A Venusian is handsome, graceful, full of joy, happiness, love and sympathy. He is a person of aesthetic taste, and remains completely engrossed in fun and enjoyment. He has no time for religion, except lip-service.

Venus is also called *Kalatra Karka*, i.e., significator for marriage. A Venusian generally marries early and leads a happy married life. If ever unmarried, his private life will not be above board. When Venus and 7th house (marriage) are afflicted by malefics (conjunction or aspect), the native becomes a reckless profligate who satisfies his physical passions somehow or the other, and also suffers due to over indulgence.

According to Hindu mythology, *Shukra* (*Acharya of Asuras*) was blinded in one eye by Lord Vishnu during *Vaman Avatar*. If Venus is not well-posited and is afflicted, the eyes will be affected. Venus when afflicted by Saturn and Ketu causes skin trouble, as it is also *karka* for beauty of the skin.

The highest exaltation degree of Venus is 27° in Pisces sign owned by Jupiter, in *Revati Nakshatra* owned by Mercury. Pisces is the last sign of the Zodiac and represents detachment from worldly pleasures after testing them, and leads to *moksha*. In Pisces, the sensuality of Venus gets disciplined, restrained and chastened under the *Satwik* (virtuous) influence of Jupiter and discrimination of Mercury. This setting keeps sensual enjoyment within limit and the humanitarian qualities of love, sympathy and compassion become more prominent.

Venus becomes deeply debilitated at 27° in the opposite sign of Virgo, which is the negative sign of Mercury, in *Chitra Nakshatra* owned by Mars. As Mercury and Venus are natural friends and Virgo is an Earthy and Movable sign, Venus ordinarily should not give bad result when in Virgo. But its location in *Chitra Nakshatra* ruled by Mars excites the Venusian sensuous character. The changeable nature of Virgo and its imaginative lord Mercury also give a fillip to Venusian indulgence. Hence, the debilitation of Venus in Virgo is quite logical.

Jupiter

The Vedic name of Jupiter is '*Brihaspati*'. '*Brihat*' means large and '*Pati*' means protector. Jupiter is the most benefic planet. In mythology, Jupiter is called *Deva Guru* or preceptor of *Devatas*. As *Guru*, Jupiter confers wisdom, learning and intellectual achievements. In the horoscope of females, Jupiter is significator for husband. According to the dictum *'Sthan hani karoti jiva'*, Jupiter harms the affairs of the house where it is located, but the houses/planets aspected by it prosper. As significator of progeny it refers to son in particular.

The highest exaltation degree of Jupiter is 5° in Cancer sign, which is 5th from Jupiterian sign Pisces. The 5th house denotes intelligence, success, fame and *Purva punya*. The highest exaltation degree falls in *Pushya Nakshatra*. In Cancer, a benefic sign owned by Moon, the spiritual wisdom of Jupiter gets a boost and makes the native an idealist and philosopher. *Pushya Nakshatra* lord Saturn denotes *Samadhi*. The changeability of Moon does not disturb the spirituality of Jupiter in *Pushya Nakshatra*. However, Jupiter's increased ethical and philosophical nature proves detrimental for material progress. Such a person becomes averse to material gains either for self or the family. This characteristics is pronounced when exalted Jupiter is located in *Kendra* or *Kona* in the horoscope. An exalted Jupiter in the 7th house generally inclines a person to celibacy, as the individual considers marriage and family a burden.

The Moon, lord of Cancer sign, is a weak dispositor for exalted Jupiter. For Sagittarius *Lagna*, Jupiter's claim to exaltation becomes blemished with location in the 8th house. Pisces *Lagna* in that respect is better, as Jupiter occupies the 5th house from it. Despite this, it suffers from the *dictum 'Karko bhava nasaya'*. However, it is considered advantageous to have an exalted Jupiter irrespective of its placement, because then it unfolds humanitarian qualities of the individual.

Jupiter's deepest debilitation degree is 5° in Capricorn ruled by Saturn and in *Uttarashada Nakshatra* ruled by the Sun. While Saturn is cold, self-centered and miserly, Jupiter is warm-hearted, kind and charitable. Capricorn is the 10th sign of natural Zodiac governing profession, position, prestige and status in life. *Nakshatra* lord Sun also represents power and authority. Jupiter's nature does not fit in this worldly and materialistic surrounding. Its placement in Capricorn does accentuate materialistic tendencies, but only through honest means and hard work. As Jupiter loses much of its virtuous qualities in Capricorn, it is considered debilitated here.

Saturn

Saturn is the farthest planet from the Sun in our solar system. In Indian mythology, Saturn has been assigned the role of *'Judge of human actions'* and dispenses justice (reward or punishment) to individuals according to their deeds. Saturn's distant location from Sun affects its movement. Due to slow motion it is also called *mandah*. Saturn (*Shani*) is described as "*Shaneh Shaneh charati iti Shaneshcharah*" (one who moves slowly). Due to its slow motion Saturn is *karka* (significator) for longevity. In the 8th house it increases longevity, as an exception to the dictum '*Karko bhava nasaya*'. As per another dictum '*Sthan Vriddhi Karoti Mandah*', Saturn gradually augments through hard work the affairs of the house it occupies in a horoscope, and harms the affairs of the houses aspected by it. Being away from the Sun (heat and light), Saturn is cold, dark in complexion, lean, miserly, introvert, melancholic, lacking in warmth and happiness. If Saturn is afflicted in the horoscope, the native becomes avaricious, deceitful and conspirator. Thus Saturn stands for paucity, restriction, poverty, and turns one to religious pursuits in the end. The effect of Saturn is experienced late in life, generally after 36 years. Being cold, calculative and *Karka* for 6th, 8th and 12th (evil) houses, Saturn causes lingering chronic diseases like paralysis, rheumatism, asthma, neurosis, constipation, tuberculosis, etc.

Saturn is exalted in Libra. In the natural Zodiac, Libra happens to be the 10th sign from Capricorn and 9th sign from Aquarius, the two signs ruled by Saturn. The 10th and 9th houses are the most powerful *Kendra* and *Trikona* houses in a horoscope. Saturn's highest exaltation degree is 20° in Libra sign, the positive sign of Venus, in *Swati Nakshatra*, ruled by Rahu. Venus lord of Libra sign, and Rahu, the *Nakshatra* lord, are friend of Saturn (*Shani vat Rahu*). Rahu is as much a factor for adversity as Saturn. The miserly, selfish and dry Saturn becomes considerably liberal in benevolent and sympathetic Venusian sign. The caution and prudence of Saturn gain width of vision and make the native somewhat benevolent and charitable. In the friendly *Nakshatra* of Rahu, Saturn does not forget its basic nature. When a poor man does not become proud on becoming rich, it is a rare virtue. An exalted Saturn in Libra *Lagna* over the period confers on the individual high position, fame and comforts in life.

Saturn is in deep debilitation at 20° in Aries, the Positive and Fiery sign of Mars, it's bitter enemy. Saturn in *Bharni Nakshatra* ruled by Venus becomes cynical and foolhardy. Saturn's association with Mars and Venus combined effect produces sinful nature. Hence, debilitation of Saturn in Aries is also justified.

Rahu and Ketu

During its movement around the earth, the orbit of Moon intersects the path of the Sun (Ecliptic) at two points which are exactly 180° apart. When the intersection occurs during the Moon's motion from South to North, it is called ascending or North Node (Rahu). When the intersection occurs during the Moon's motion from North to South, the intersection point is called the descending or Southern Node (Ketu). When the new Moon (on *Amavasya*) is within 5° from this nodal point, it intercepts the light of the Sun from reaching the earth and the phenomenon is called Solar Eclipse. The degree of proximity of the Moon to the Node determines the extent of the eclipse. When the full Moon (on *Purnima*) crosses the nodal point, the shadow of the earth falls on the Moon and causes Lunar Eclipse. As the only apparent phenomenon that can be connected with Rahu and Ketu are the eclipses, when shadow (*Chhaya*) obscures the Sun or the Moon, our visionary *Rishis* called these as '*Chhayagraha*' or shadowy planets.

The Western astrologers have named Rahu and Ketu as Dragon's Head and Dragon's Tail respectively, thereby revealing their origin from the Hindu mythology. They consider Rahu as benefic and Ketu as malefic, while Indian authorities regard both Rahu and Ketu as *tamsik* (malefic) in nature. Rahu is often described as giving the result similar to Saturn as per dictum '*Shani vat Rahu*'. However, while Saturn is cool, calculative and secretive, Rahu is ambitious, practical and confrontist, and believes in achieving the goal by hook or crook.

Ketu is said to give result similar to Mars – '*Kuja vat Ketu*'. However, while Mars is active and argumentative, Ketu is psychic

Rationale of Exaltation of Planets

and mystical. Rahu is considered powerful in the first six signs of the Zodiac (from Aries to Virgo), while Ketu is strong in the last six signs (from Libra to Pisces).

Rahu has *Rajasik* relationship with Venus, friendly relationship with Saturn, and spoils Mercury and Jupiter. The Sun, Moon and Mars are Rahu's enemies. Ketu has *Satvik* relationship with Jupiter and is friendly to the Sun, Moon and Mars. It is neutral to Mercury, while Venus and Saturn are its enemies. Some astrological works assign 5th, 7th, 9th and 12th houses full aspect to Rahu and Ketu from their locations, while others deny this on the ground that the Nodes are only mathematical points without any mass, volume or light.

As malefics, Rahu and Ketu give good result when posited in 3rd, 6th and 11th houses of the horoscope. When well-posited in the horoscope, and associated with or aspected by benefics and *Yogakarka* planets, they give good result in the matter of finance and prosperity during their *Dasa-Bhukti*. Rahu (like Saturn) gives chronic diseases depending on its location, aspect and association with malefics, and Ketu (like Mars) causes injury, operation and even death.

The majority of Indian authorities have assigned Virgo as own sign to Rahu, Aquarius as its *Mooltrikona* sign, Gemini as its exaltation sign, and Sagittarius as the debilitation sign. Pisces is considered as own sign of Ketu, Leo as its *Mooltrikona* sign, Sagittarius as its exaltation sign, and Gemini as its sign of debilitation. Some authorities consider Taurus as the exaltation sign of Rahu and Scorpio as the exaltation sign of Ketu. The opposite sign Scorpio becomes the debilitation sign of Rahu and Taurus as debilitation sign of Ketu.

Assignment of Gemini as exaltation sign to Rahu appears more logical. Rahu is sensitive in nature and acts as a catalyst in fructification of good or bad events in human life. Gemini is an Airy sign owned by intelligent and volatile Mercury. Moreover, Gemini contains the full *Nakshatra Aridra*, owned by Rahu and three *Padas* of Punarvasu (Jupiter). Rahu has neutral relationship with Jupiter and Mercury. Rahu is scientific, practical and quite comfortable in Gemini It gives the best result when posited in own *Nakshatra Aridra* from 6° 40' to 20° in Gemini. Similarly, Aquarius, ruled by Saturn, the *Mooltrikona* sign is also an Airy and Intellectual sign, and contains Rahu's full *Nakshatra Satabisha,* and three- fourth of *Purvabhadrapada Nakshatra* owned by Jupiter. In the light of the above details the own, *Mooltrikona* and exaltation signs allotted to Ketu, just opposite to Rahu, also hold good.

According to Hindu Karma Theory, Rahu connotes the culmination of past sins committed within the family, which are working themselves out in this life of the individual, whose destiny is linked with the family. On the other hand, Ketu is the means through which this family curse or destiny can be altered by intelligent and constructive efforts directed into wholesome channels for attaining liberation after the *Prarabdha* (result of past *Karma*) is exhausted in the shape of destiny. Ketu is, therefore, called *Mokshakarka*.

The preceding elaboration shows that the exaltation signs and degree assigned to different planets is based on sound logic and valid rationale.

Any planet posited in the same sign in *Navamsa* chart is called *Vargottam* and gains additional strength to do good. Besides, when Mars, Mercury, Jupiter, Venus and Saturn (each of these) occupy a *Kendra*, in own or exaltation sign, these respectively form five *Pancha Mahapurusha Yogas*-namely, *Ruchuk*, *Bhadra*, *Hamsa*, *Malavya* and *Sasa Yoga* which confer high status, success and fame to the native in life. These five *Yogas* are also operative when counted from the Moon *Lagna*, which is equated to *Lagna* (Ascendant), and bestows to the native wealth and supremacy. According to *Phaladeepika*:

त्र्याद्यै: खेटै: स्वोच्चगै: केन्द्रसंस्थै: स्वर्क्षस्थैर्वा भूपति स्यात्प्रसिद्ध: ।

(Ch. 7,1)

meaning, "If a native has in his birth chart three or more planets in their exaltation or own sign and at the same time occupying *Kendra*, he becomes widely renowned like a king."

The classics, however, put a rider that:

नृपकुले कुरूतो नृपमन्यथा द्रविडपं परितो भवतो नरम्।

Rationale of Exaltation of Planets

meaning, "The native of a royal family born with *Rajyogas* becomes a King, and if born in any other family, he becomes owner of much wealth."

Experience shows that the result produced by an exalted planet is relative to individual's family background and enterprise. The result also depends on the planet's nearness to its highest degree of exaltation and its position in *Navamsa* and *Bhava Chalit* Charts. This is amply demonstrated in the following example horoscopes.

1. Male, DOB: 23.10.1954, 11.37 P.M., Bulandshahar (UP).

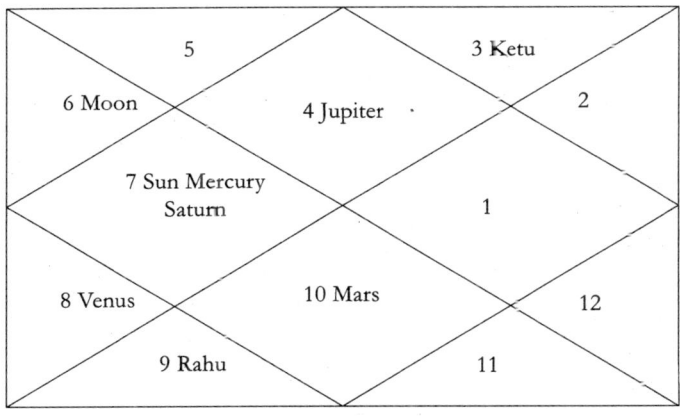

Jupiter, Saturn and Mars, exalted in *Kendra*, form *Hamsa*, *Sasa*, and *Ruchuk Mahapurusha Yogas*. There is also *Buddha-Aditya Yoga* in the 4th house with cancellation of debilitation of the Sun.

The native was born in a middle class family and completed his C.A. in record time with good divison. At the start of Jupiter *Dasa* in 1992 he got an opening in a Dubai based MNC. He is head of Accounts Division drawing handsome pay package.

Saturn *Dasa* will confer further heights on the individual.

2. Male, DOB: 8.9.1955, 0405 AM, Mumbai.

5 Mars Venus Sun	3	2 Moon Ketu
6 Merc	4 Jupiter	
7 Saturn		1
8 Rahu	10	12
	9	11

		Moon Ketu	
			Lagna Jupiter
			Mars Sun Venus
	Rahu	Saturn	Mercury

Rationale of Exaltation of Planets

Jupiter, Saturn, Mercury and Moon are exalted and the Sun is in own sign. Apparently, the horoscope appears quite strong. Jupiter forms *Hamsa Yoga* in *Lagna* and Saturn forms *Sasa Yoga* in 4th house.

On closer examination it is seen that Saturn is lord of 7th and 8th house and its dispositor Venus is combust. Jupiter is aspected by Rahu and Saturn. Mercury is the lord of 3rd and 12th house. Moon is afflicted in Rahu-Ketu axis. *Yogakarka* Mars and Venus are combust in 2nd house. In *Navamsa* Chart Sun and Saturn are debilitated and opposed to each other, and Jupiter is in inimical sign.

The native's Jupiter *Dasa* started from November, 1993 without giving the result of *Hamsa Yoga* and the native faced financial problems. The Jupiter *dasa* coincided with *Sade-sati*, and Saturn transited over *Dasa* lord Jupiter, over Sun in 2nd house, and also caused *Sheni Dhaiya* upto September 10, 2009. Though, *dasa* lord Jupiter transited through own *Mooltrikona* sign, but through 8th from Moon and in 6th from *Lagna* upto December 9, 2008. *Dasa-Chidra* (Jupiter-Rahu) runs upto November, 2009.

The next *Dasa* lord Saturn is debilitated in *Navamsa* and opposed by Sun there. Its *Dasa* may not give the expected result of *Sasa Yoga*. The horoscope shows that an exalted planet if afflicted does not produce expected benefic result, and adverse transit adds to the suffering.

3. Male, DOB: 1.10.1934, 2.49 A.M., Jhansi (UP).

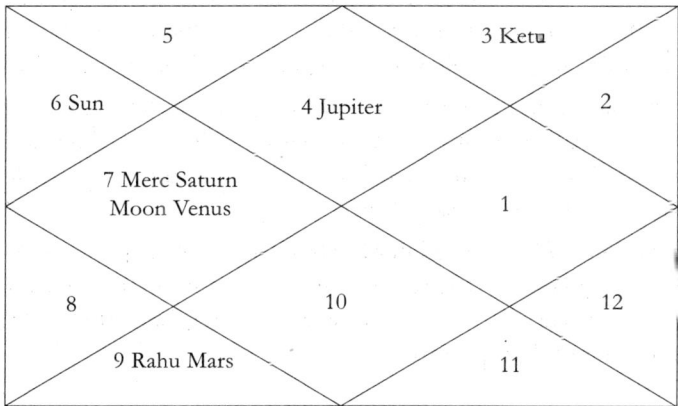

			Ketu
			Lagna Jupiter
Rahu Mars		Merc. Saturn Moon Venus	Sun

Jupiter is exalted in *Lagna* and *Vargottam* in *Navamsa*. Saturn is exalted in 4th house (Libra). Venus is in own sign in 4th house. These form *Hamsa, Sasa* and *Malavya Panch Mahapurusha Yogas*. Jupiter in *Kendra* to Moon also forms *Gajkesari Yoga*. Apparently, the horoscope looks impressive.

On deeper scrutiny it transpires that most of the planets are on left side in a male horoscope. *Lagna* lord Moon is weak (*Pakshabalheen*) being in 2nd to the Sun. It is located with Saturn and suffers from *Udarastha Sade-sati*. Saturn is malefic lord of 7th and 8th houses and is conjoined with 3rd and 12th lord Mercury. The planets in 4th house are afflicted by debilitated Ketu from 12th house. Jupiter is 6th and 9th lord exalted in *Lagna*. It is aspected by Mars which is itself afflicted by Rahu in 6th house. Jupiter is also aspected by 7th and 8th lord Saturn.

The native had Juptier *Dasa* balance of about 8 ½ years at birth followed by unfavourable *Dasa* of Saturn (19 years), Mercury (17 years), and Ketu (7 years) which covered his youth and middle age and deprived him success in life.

His Venus *Dasa* started in March, 2006. In *Navamsa* Chart Venus is *Bhava Vargottam* as it remains in 4th house Libra and shows some respite. However, his *Sade-sati* will start in September, 2009 and cause frustration and disappointment.

Rationale of Exaltation of Planets

This horoscope also shows that exalted planets do not produce expected result when these have bad lordship, are afflicted, coupled with unfavourable transit and *Dasa* sequence

RECAPITULATION

The planets give good result in decreasing order when in exaltation, *Mooltrikona*, own sign and friendly sign. An exalted planet gives good result commensurate with its nearness to the highest degree of exaltation. It should not be afflicted by malefics, or debilitated in *Navamsa,* and other *Varga* Charts. The good results given by an exalted planet is relative to individual's family background and enterprise.

The result given by a debilitated or combust planet is disappointing. In the following situation a debilitated or combust planet gives some good result:-

1. A debilitated planet when *Vargottam* in *Navamsa* Chart gives some good result.
2. Though some potential *Raj Yogas* arising from debilitated as well as retrograde planets are cited in Astrological treatises, yet majority view is that an exalted or debilitated planet does not give contrary result in retrogression.
3. A debilitated *Lagna* lord in retrogression remains a benefic.
4. A combust planet loses most of the results of the house it occupies, but retains some of the effect pertaining to the house ruled or aspected by it if it is associated with other strong planets. Mercury loses the least of its benevolent effect when combust.

Chapter IV
Lagna and *Bhava* Charts

The *Lagna* Chart prepared for the time and place of birth of an individual indicates the rising sign with its degree, and planetary position in the 12 signs (*Rasis*) of the Zodiac. The *Bhava Chart* is prepared by taking *Lagna* degree as the midpoint of the first *Bhava* and the planets are placed cuspwise in different *Bhavas*. The 12 *Bhavas* represent different facets of human life as under:

तनुर्धनश्च भ्राता च सुहृत्पुत्र-रिपुः स्त्रियः ।
मृत्युश्च धर्मकर्माय - व्यया भावाः प्रकीर्तिताः ॥

meaning, "The body, wealth, brother, relatives, progeny, enemy, wife, death, religion, livelihood, gains, and loss are respectively the significations of first to the 12th *Bhava*."

In Vedic Astrology, the rising degree of the *Lagna* is taken as the mid-point of the first house (*Bhava*), which extends about 15° backward and 15° forward from mid-point, depending upon the place of birth. While the 12 *Rasis* (signs) of the zodiac have a fixed span of 30° each, *Bhavas* may be a little more or less than 30°. The *Bhava* Chart is useful in making precise prediction. When the location of planets in *Lagna* Chart changes in *Bhava* Chart, these prominently give the result of their *Bhava* position, and indicate how the position evident from *Lagna* Chart changes in future.

The *Lagna* (*Rasi*) Chart and *Bhava* (house) Chart are usually different because *Bhava* Chart is made by taking *Lagna* degree as the middle point of first *Bhava*. When the *Lagna spasht* (mid-point of 1st *Bhava*) is at the beginning or towards the end of a *Rasi* (sign), then the planets change their location in *Bhava* Chart. When the *Lagna*

Lagna and Bhava Charts

spasht is near mid-point of a sign, and the planets are located between 5° to 25°, then the *Lagna* and *Bhava* Charts are almost identical as is evident from the following horoscopes.

1. Male, DOB: 14.9.1938, 23.36 hrs., Jhansi (UP).

Lagna Chart

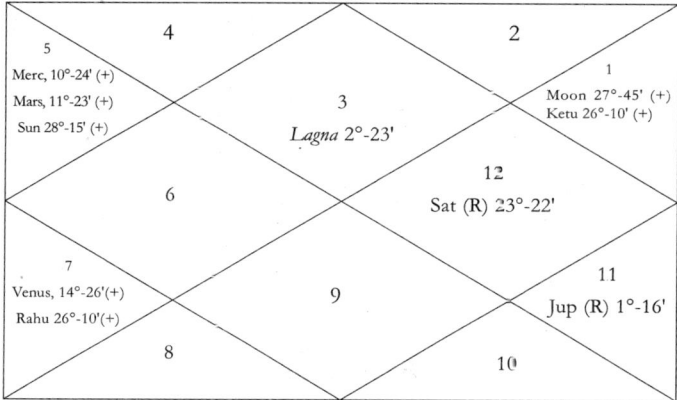

Bhava Chart

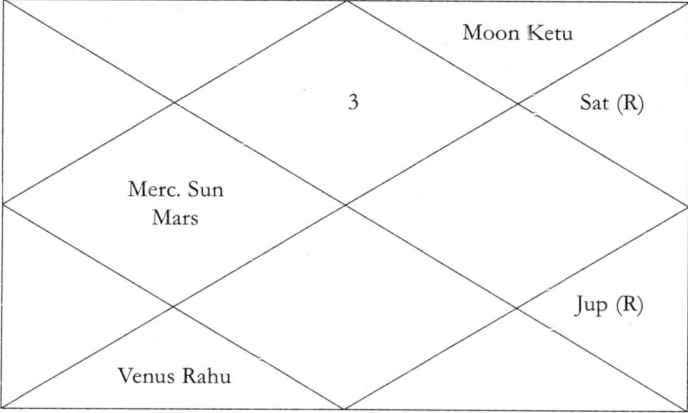

Lagna Chart

	Ketu 26°-10'(+) Moon 27°-45'(+)		*Langa* 2°-23'
Sat (R) 23°-22'(+)			
Jup (R) 1°-16'			
			Merc.10°-24'(+) Mars 11°-23'(+) Sun 28°-15'(+)
		Venus, 14°-26'(+) Rahu 26°-10'(+)	

Bhava Chart

	Sat (R)	Moon Ketu	*Lagna*
Jap (R)			
	Venus Rahu		Merc Sun Mars

The *Lagna spasht* is 2° 23', which is near the beginning of Gemini sign. Except Jupiter all other planets have changed their location in *Bhava* Chart.

2. Male, DOB: 17.6.1969, 03.30 hrs., Jorhat (Assam).

Lagna Chart

	Sun 2°-7' Moon 23°-24' 3	Merc. 11°-29' Lagna 20°-24' 2	Venus 16°-25' Sat 12°-8' 1 12 Rahu 2°-48'
4	5		11
6 Ketu 2°-48' Jup. 3°-34'	7	8 Mars (R) 11°-22' 9	10

Bhava Chart

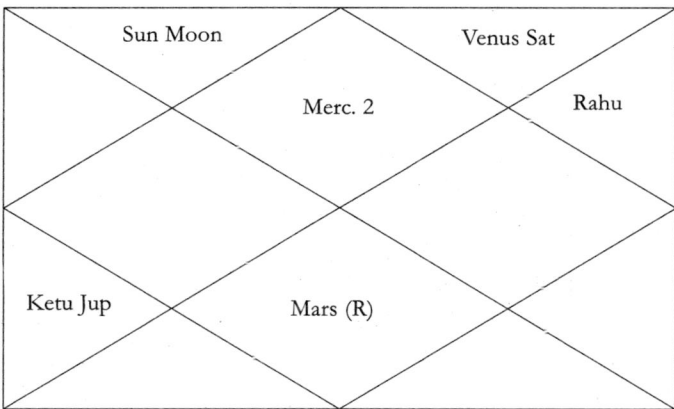

Lagna Chart

Rahu 2°-48'	Sat 12°-8' Venus, 16°-25'	Lagna 20°-24' Merc. 11°-29'	Sun 2°-7' Moon 23°-24'
	Mars (R) 11°-32'		Ketu 2°-48' Jup 3°-34'

Bhava Chart

Rahu	Sat. Venus	Lagna Merc.	Sun Moon
Jup (R) 1-16°			
	Mars (R)		Ketu Jup

The *Lagna spasht* is 20° 24' which is near the middle of Taurus sign. There is no change in the two charts.

Lagna and Bhava Charts

In North India *Lagna* Chart the *Rasis* are indicated by their number, for example, Aries – 1, Taurus -2, Gemini -3, and so on. The numbers are, however, not indicated in *Bhava* Chart which shows the *Bhava* location of planets. In South India Chart *Rasi* numbers are not mentioned as the *Rasi* Chart is treated fixed and *Lagna* is indicated in the sign it falls. It may be reiterated that when there is change in *Bhava* position, a planet does not change its *Rasi* position.

In some computer generated horoscopes when a planet changes it position in *Bhava* Chart, say from 5th house to 6th house, then a (+) mark is inscribed on the planet in *Lagna* chart, which indicates that the planet has shifted to the next *Bhava*. When the planet goes to previous house, it is indicated by a (-) mark on the planet, which conveys that the planet has shifted to the previous *Bhava*. The computer programmes save much time and labour involved in erection of correct *Lagna* and *Bhava* Charts.

The *Bhava* Chart is quite important, but it is not a substitute for *Lagna* Chart which remains the basic chart. Though earlier *Rishis* did not discuss *Bhava* Chart, its importance has been highlighted by later *Acharyas*. Experience also shows that for precision in prediction the assessment from *Lagna* Chart has to be suitably modified in accordance with the changed planetary position in *Bhava* Chart. Judgment about the extent of modification depends on the expertise and experience of the astrologer. The importance and utility of *Bhava* Chart will be clear from the horoscope of two distinguished persons discussed below.

1. Smt. Indira Gandhi, former P.M. of India,
DOB: 19.11.1917, 23.11 hrs., Allahabad (UP).

Lagna Chart

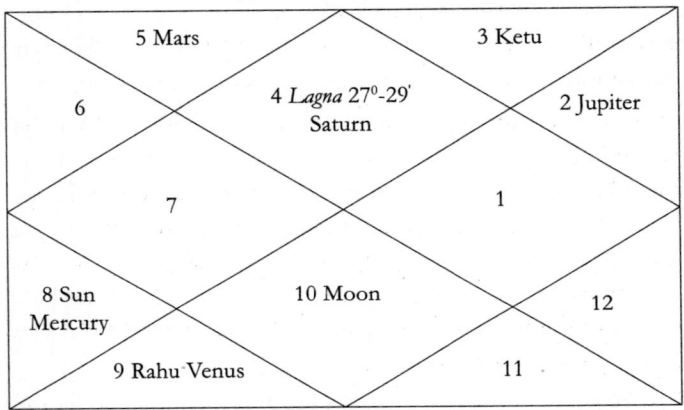

Bhava Chart

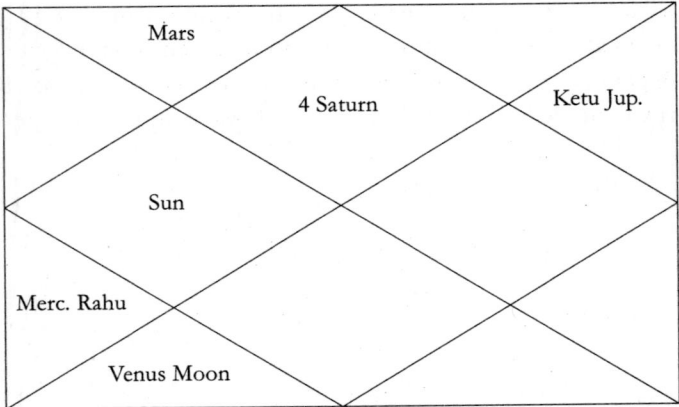

Lagna Chart

		Jupiter	Ketu
			Lagna 27°-29' Saturn
Moon			Mars
Rahu Venus	Sun Mercury		

Bhava Chart

		Jupiter Ketu	
			Lagna Saturn
			Mars
Venus Moon	Mercury Rahu	Sun	

The *Bhava* Chart shows four changes from *Lagna* Chart. The Sun goes to 4th *Bhava* from 5th, Rahu goes to 5th *Bhava* from 6th, Moon shift to 6th *Bhava* from 7th and Ketu shifts to the 11th *Bhava* from 12th.

The *Lagna spasht* is Cancer 27° 29', and the first *Bhava* starts from 12° 4' Cancer. The 7th *Bhava* starts from 12° 4' Capricorn and ends at 12° 4' Aquarius. The *Lagna* lord Moon is in Capricorn (5° 35') in the 7th house, but is relegated to 6th in *Bhava* Chart. While the *Lagna* lord Moon assimilates the characteristics of Capricorn sign, such as dominating nature, whimsical, and organizational skill, it is also influenced by the characteristics of 6th *Bhava* in *Bhava* Chart. Here, 6th *Bhava* does not mean Sagittarius sign, but only the properties and significations of 6th house. Likewise, the Sun in Scorpio at 4° 7' shifts to 5th *Bhava*. The 2nd lord Sun acquires the characteristics of the sign Scorpio in *Lagna* chart together with those of the 4th *Bhava* in *Bhava* Chart. The 4th house falls in Libra but while interpreting the result, the Sun is to be treated as occupying the 4th in Scorpio. Though the native was born to high status parents, the shifting of *Matru Karka* Moon to 6th *Bhava* and the Sun (*Karka* for father) to 4th *Bhava*, denied her parental happiness during childhood, as mother remained sick and father remained in and out of jail during Independence struggle.

In *Lagna* Chart the 7th lord Saturn is in *Lagna*, and *Lagna* lord Moon is in the 7th. Their mutual exchange should normally give happy married life. But Saturn by its nature delayed the marriage. Shifting of Moon from 7th to 6th in *Bhava* Chart created coldness in relationship after some time. As the mutual position of *Lagna* lord Moon and 7th lord Saturn in *Bhava* chart changed to malefic *Shashtashtaka* (6/8) position, it also caused early demise of her husband.

In *Navamsa* Chart the 7th lord Mercury is located in 8th and conjoins 8th lord Venus. It is afflicted by Saturn and Rahu. This planetary position also corroborates the fact of widowhood.

There is *Mahabhagya Yoga* formed by *Lagna*, Moon and the Sun being in even sign in night birth for female native in *Lagna* Chart. Though, the Sun and the Moon change houses in *Bhava* chart, yet it did no affect the *Yoga* result formed in *Lagna* Chart and she remained Prime Minsiter of India for record number of years.

The *Lagna* is in *Pap kartari Yoga*. The 8th lord Saturn is in *Lagna* in an inimical sign. Incendiary planets Mars and Ketu aspect 8th house. This planetary position was responsible for her assassination in

Saturn-Rahu *Dasa*. Rahu is debilitated in 6th house and the *Dasa* and *Bhukti* lords are located *Shahtashtak* (6/8) to each other.

2. Adolf Hitler,

   DOB: 20.4.1889, 6.30 P.M., Brabhaw (Germany).

Lagna Chart

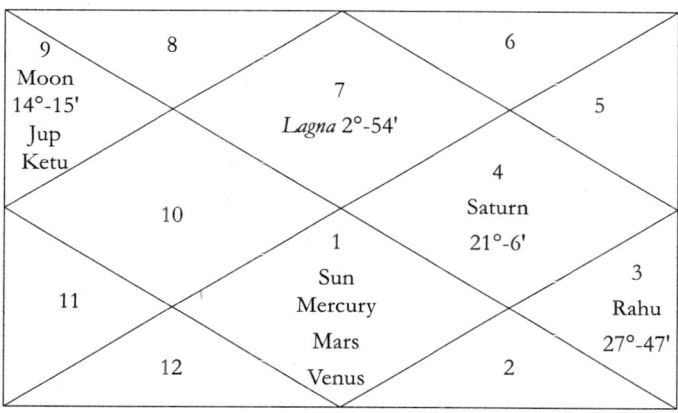

Bhava Chart

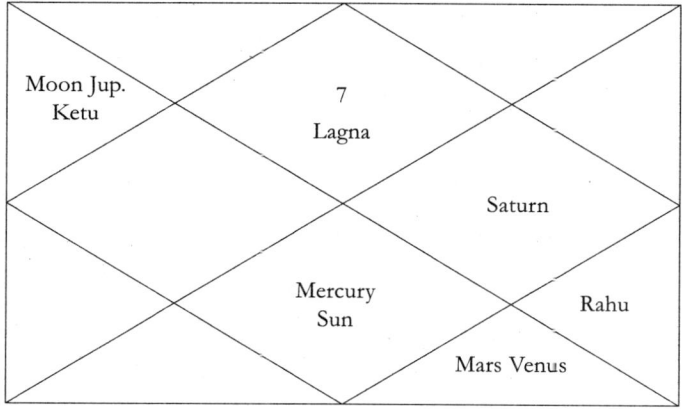

Lagna Chart

	Sun Merc. Mars Venus		Rahu 27°-47'
			Sat. 21°-6'
Moon 14°-15' Jup Ketu		Lagna 2°-54'	

Bhava Chart

	Merc. Sun	Mars Venus	Rahu
			Saturn
Moon Jup. Ketu		Lagna	

The *Lagna* Chart has following *Yogas*.
1. *Ruchuk Yoga* - Mars occupies own sign Aries in *Kendra*.
2. *Lakshmi Yoga* - *Lagna* lord Venus and 9th lord Mercury are conjoined in *Kendra*.
3. *Mahabhagya Yoga* - The *Lagna*, Moon and Sun occupy odd signs, namely Libra, Sagittarius and Aries respectively, in male horoscope during day birth.
4. *Gajkesari Yoga* - The Moon and Jupiter are conjoined in Sagittarius, but afflicted by Rahu – Ketu axis.

In *Bhava* Chart Mars and Venus shift to 8th house from 7th house and destroy *Ruchuk Yoga* and *Lakshmi Yoga*. But this change did not destroy the effect of *Yogas*, formed in *Lagna* Chart. *Ruchuk Yoga* made him an aggressive leader with great following, and *Lakshmi Yoga* made him very rich. *Gajkesari Yoga* gave him high status, fame and oratory skill to captivate his audience. *Mahabhagya Yoga* made him one of the most powerful leader of his time.

The aspect of Mars, Venus, Mercury and the Sun from 7th house on Libra *Lagna* greatly influenced his personality, character, attitude and behaviour. The aspect of Mars on the 10th house points to his military career. The Moon-Jupiter conjunction which formed *Gajakesari Yoga* was converted into *Guru-Chandala Yoga* due to Rahu-Ketu influence and created in him fanatical hatred for the Jews.

Going both by *Lagna* and *Bhava* Charts, either by the presence of Mars, Venus, Sun and Mercury in 7th (Aries) aspected by Saturn in *Lagna* Chart, or only Sun and Mercury in 7th *Bhava* aspected by Saturn in *Bhava* Chart, indicate much digression in private life.

The location of *Yogakarka* Saturn in 10th house in inimical sign in *Lagna* Chart gave him spectacular rise in his career followed by tragic end. In *Lagna* Chart Saturn in 10th *Bhava* has mutual aspect with Mars posited in 7th, which is very inauspicious for career and longevity. In *Bhava Chart* Mars shifts to 8th house which disturbs mutual aspect with Saturn, yet their inauspicious mutual aspect in *Lagna* Chart gave its result in full measure and he committed suicide by shooting himself. The result of *Yogas* and planetary location in *Lagna* Chart produced their result in full measure.

The gist of above discussion is as follows:
1. *Lagna* and *Bhava* Chart indications should be judiciously blended for making accurate prediction.
2. Planets which change position in *Bhava* Chart from *Lagna* Chart modify their result, which tilts towards their *Bhava* position.
3. *Yogas* are considered only from *Lagna* Chart. Change of planetary position in *Bhava* Chart apparently may destroy the *Yogas* formed in *Lagna* Chart, but this does not affect *Yoga* result. The changed planetary position in *Bhava* Chart does not form any new *Yoga*.
4. Aspects are also primarily seen in *Lagna* Chart.
5. Benefic planets in *Kendras* in *Lagna* Chart give strength to the horoscope. Their shifting to non-*Kendra* position in *Bhava* Chart does not reduce the strength of the horoscope. Conversely, malefics in *Kendras* in *Lagna* Chart show a life of struggle and suffering. A change in location of malefics to non-*Kendra* position in *Bhava* Chart does not improve the quality of life.

Chapter V

Inter-relationship of Sign, *Bhava* and Planets

Astrology is both a science and an art. It is a science because its calculation part is based on pure Astronomy and Mathematics. It is an art, as after acquiring thorough knowledge of the Vedic science of astrology, and applying its principles on a large number of horoscopes, an astrologer acquires confidence and refinement in predicting future.

It is the basic tenet of astrology that different constituent factors, namely, the *Rasi* (Sign), *Bhava* (House) and *Nakshatra* (Constellation), imprint their influence on the planets located in the birth chart, and the resultant effect is experienced during their *Dasa-Bhukti*. The planets constantly transit through the zodiac.

The 12 houses (*Bhava*) of the horoscope indicate different facets of human life from birth to death as under:

देहो द्रव्यपराक्रमौ सुख सुतौ शत्रु:कलत्रं मृतिभग्यं
राज्यपदं क्रमेण गदिता लाभव्ययौ लग्नत:

meaning, "The 12 houses of the horoscope starting from *Lagna* are called *Deh* (body), *Dhana* (wealth), *Parakram* (endeavour), *Sukh* (comforts), *Putra* (progeny/son), *Shatru* (enemy), *Kalatra* (spouse), *Mritih* (death/longevity), *Bhagya* (luck), *Rajya* (Rank/status), *Labh* (gain), and *Vyaya* (loss)." The 6th, 8th and 12th house are called *Dushtsthana* (evil houses) and their association in any form is harmful. Among these 8th house and its lord are regarded most malefic. The remaining houses are considered good houses. The 1st, 4th, 7th and 10th houses are called *Kendra* (Quadrants), and 1st, 5th and 9th houses are called *Trikona* (Trines). The *Trikona* houses are always auspicious, and when occupied by benefics these become more strong. *Trikona* lords give good result during their *Dasa-Bhukti*. *Lagna* being simultaneously a *Kendra* and *Trikona*, its lord always gives good result unless weak or afflicted. The *Lagna* lord indicates in brief the potential or grade of the horoscope. The lord of 2nd and 12th houses gives the result of the other house owned by it, otherwise like the planet it associates. (स्थानान्तरानगुण्येन भवत: फलदायकौ।)

Location of every planet in a sign modifies its inherent quality and effect. When a planet is located in a particular sign and attains maximum strength it is called 'exalted'. The Sun in Aries, Moon in Taurus, Mercury in Virgo, Jupiter in Cancer, Venus in Pisces, Mars in Capricorn, and Saturn in Libra, are exalted and have maximum strength when free from any other malefic influence. Conversely, the planets lack in strength when these occupy just opposite sign (7th to their exaltation sign), and are considered debilitated.

According to their characteristics Jupiter and Venus are natural benefics without any condition. Sun is regarded a cruel planet. Moon is treated as benefic when it is more than 72° away from the Sun, both in dark and bright fortnight. Mercury when acting alone is benefic, but in the company, or influence, of malefics it acts as malefic. Mars, Saturn, Rahu and Ketu are natural malefics. Rahu acts like Saturn, while Ketu acts like Mars. (शनिवद्राहु: कुजवत्केतु:।)

Planets as lord of *Kendra* cease to be natural benefic or natural malefic as the case may be. The lords of *Trikona* house whether natural benefic or natural malefic always give good result. Lords of 3rd, 6th and 11th houses give bad result. The lords of 6th, 8th and 12th houses give malefic result.

In keeping with the inherent nature and relationship of their lord with other planets, the signs are considered friendly, inimical or neutral to different planets. A planet is very strong in the sign of exaltation, it is less strong in its *Mooltrikona* sign, and a little less strong

Inter-relationship of Sign, Bhava and Planets

in own sign. When a planet is located in a friend's sign it has medium strength and gives good result in respect of that house and also of the house owned by it. On the other hand, if a planet occupies an inimical sign, it not only spoils the prospects of the house where located but also of the house owned by it. The strength of a house depends on that of its lord. Benefics on both sides of a house and its lord strengthen these.

Among the 12 signs nos. 1, 3, 5, 7, 9 and 11 are odd and male signs, while sign nos. 2, 4, 6, 8, 10 and 12 are even and female in nature. Among the planets Jupiter, Sun and Mars are male planets; Venus, Moon and Rahu are female planets; and Ketu, Saturn and Mercury are regarded effeminate. When in a female horoscope *Lagna* falls in a female (even) sign, and a female planet as lord of a female sign occupies it, or aspects it, and *Lagna* lord also occupies a female sign, that female is blessed with excellent womanly grace, charm and qualities, as in the following example horoscope.

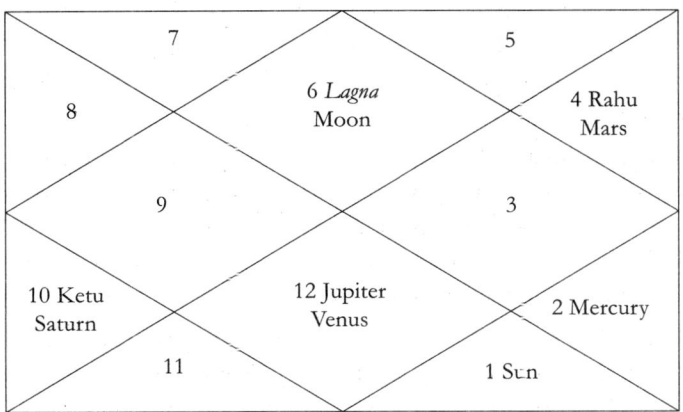

Jupiter Venus	Sun	Mercury	
			Rahu Mars
Ketu Saturn			
			Lagna Moon

Lagna falls in even sign. Its lord is posited in an even sign. *Lagna* is occupied by Moon, a female planet and is lord of a female sign. *Lagna* is aspected by exalted Venus from an even sign. Thus *Lagna*, *Lagna* lord, planet located in *Lagna* and aspecting *Lagna*, all have feminine characteristics which has made the native extremely beautiful and cultured.

Similarly, in a male horoscope when *Lagna* falls in a male sign, is aspected, or occupied, by its lord, or a male planet, and *Lagna* lord occupies a male sign, that person will have prominent male qualities of gait, appearance and conduct. Mixed sign and planetary combination produces mixed personality.

The signs have also been classified according to four elements – Fire, Earth, Air and Water. Aries, Leo and Sagittarius are Fiery; Taurus, Virgo and Capricorn are Earthy; Gemini, Libra and Aquarius are Airy; and Cancer, Scorpio and Pisces are Watery sign. Similarly, the planets have these characteristics as under:

Fiery : Sun and Mars;   Earthy : Saturn,
Airy : Mercury and Jupiter;   Watery : Moon and Venus.

A Watery planet located in a Watery sign along with or aspected by a Watery planet, would indicate predominance of Watery element.

Inter-relationship of Sign, Bhava and Planets

Similarly, a Fiery planet posited in a Fiery sign, along with, or aspected by a Fiery planet would show Fiery effect in full, and so on. These factors are helpful in predicting accident or death by water, fire, etc.

The individual of the following horoscope got his right hand burnt during childhood, but survived due to the benefic aspect of Jupiter on *Lagna* from 9th house (the house of *Deva Kripa*), on *Lagna* lord Mercury and 3rd house (right hand).

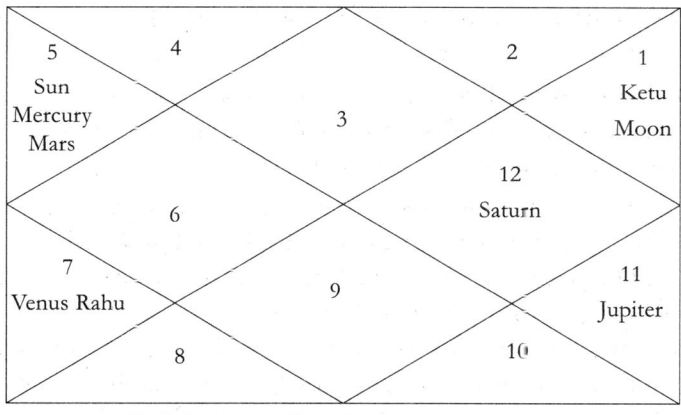

In the horoscope *Lagna* lord Mercury is in Leo in 3rd house (right hand), with Fiery planets Mars and the Sun, and aspected by Ketu. Mercury is symbolic of *Kumar* (boy).

The signs have also been classified into Movable (*Char*), Fixed (*Sthir*) and Common (*Dwiswabhava*). If the factors representing body, i.e., *Lagna*, its lord, Moon and the lord of Moon sign, the Sun and the lord of the sign occupied by the Sun, are all located in Movable sign, it would indicate frequent movement of the body of the native, i.e., who travels a lot. Majority of these in Fixed sign will give almost permanent stay at a place and in Common sign will give mixed result. The native of the horoscope given above had only three transfers during his 40 years' service.

Planets have 'nil' strength in *Bhava-Sandhi* (junction point of *Bhavas*), are weak in the first and last 6° of a sign, and give full result when located from 12° to 18° in any sign,

As discussed earlier, planets in their exaltation, *Mooltrikona*, and own signs are strong, and when also located in *Kendra* houses, these attain special positive qualities, and the resultant effect is called *Panch Mahapurusha Yoga*. Such planets uplift the individual in the sphere of activity ruled by it. Such *Yogas* are invariably present in the horoscopes of successful and wealthy persons.

Sometimes closer collaboration of houses and planets produces special effect. In the following example horoscope of a male with Virgo *Lagna*, Jupiter is exalted in Cancer in 11th house; Moon is in the 4th house and Venus in 7th house.

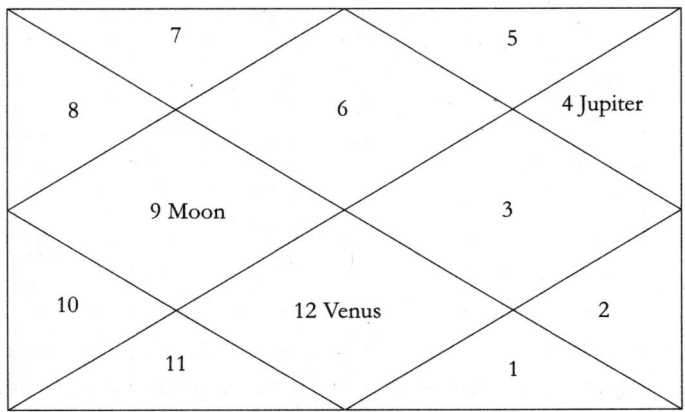

Inter-relationship of Sign, Bhava and Planets

Venus			
			Jupiter
Moon			Lagna

The 4th house being the house of mother is a female house. The 5th house is a female sign, and the 7th house (wife) in Pisces sign is again female in character. Moon and Venus (female planets) are under female elements. The resultant effect would be that a male planet Jupiter, as lord of 4th and 7th (female) houses and dispositor of female planets Moon and Venus, located in Cancer (female sign) comes under total female influence and will behave accordingly. Normally the aspect of a strong Jupiter on the 5th house of progeny assures the birth of male issues but, in the example horoscope, because of dominant female influence, it will act as a female planet and its aspect on the 5th house will produce only female issues. Such is the combined modifying effect of female houses and planets on *Putra Karka* Jupiter.

Sometimes, signs also act as planets. For example, if a person is born in Gemini *Lagna* with Sun and Mars in it, then Sun lord of 3rd house of younger brother and Mars, *Karka* for younger brother, will be influenced by the dual nature of Mercury due to their placement in Gemini *Lagna*, and the native may have a twin brother.

Every conceivable aspect of human life, as stated earlier, is represented by a specific house, its lord and *Karka* (significator). For example, the Sun is *Karka* for father. Hence, the affairs relating to father are examined from 9th house, its lord and the Sun, as *Karka* for father. The strength of *Bhava* lord is decisive as it also strengthens the *bhava* and planets located therein. The *Bhava* and *Karka* for some important affairs of life are as under.

1. Health: *Lagna*, its lord and *Karka* Sun.
2. Longevity: 1st and 8th houses, their lords and *Karka* Saturn.
3. Status: 1st and 10th houses, their lords and *Karka* Sun, Jupiter, Mercury and Saturn.
4. Wealth: 2nd and 11th houses, their lords and *Karka* Jupiter.
5. Eyes: 2nd house, its lord and *Karka* Sun for right eye. 12th house, its lord and *Karka* Moon for left eye.
6. Speech: 2nd house, its lord and *Karka* Mercury.
7. Education: 2nd and 5th houses, their lords and *Karka* Mercury, and Jupiter.
8. Brothers: 3rd house, its lord and *Karka* Mars for younger one; 11th house, its lord and *Karka* Jupiter for elder one.
9. Ears: 3rd house, its lord and *Karka* Mercury for right ear; 11th house, its lord and *Karka* Jupiter for left ear.
10. Mother: 4th house, its lord and *Karka* Moon.
11. Conveyance: 4th house, its lord and *Karka* Venus.
12. Property: 4th house, its lord and *Karka* Mars.
13. Lands: 4th house, its lord and *Karka* Saturn.
14. Comforts: 4th house, its lord and *Karka* Venus and Jupiter.
15. Son: 5th and 9th houses, their lord and *Karka* Jupiter.
16. Daughter: 5th and 9th houses, their lord and *Karka* Moon and Venus.
17. Injury/Disease: 6th house, its lord and *Karka* Mars and Saturn.
18. Wife: 2nd, 7th and 11th houses, their lord and *Karka* Venus.

19.	Husband:	2nd, 7th and 11th houses, their lord and *Karka* Jupiter.
20.	Evil deeds:	8th house, its lord and *Karka* Mars and Saturn.
21.	Religion:	9th house, its lord and *Karka* Jupiter.
22.	Father:	9th house, its lord and *Karka* Sun.
23.	Profession:	2nd, 6th and 10th houses, their lord and *Karka* Sun, Jupiter, Mercury and Saturn.
24.	Gains and elder brother	11th house, its lord and *Karka* Jupiter.
25.	Sleep and bed comforts:	12th house, its lord and *Karka* Venus.
26.	Foreign travel:	3rd, 9th and 12th houses, their lords, and *Karka* Saturn and Rahu.

The conjunction or aspect of benefics on a house, its lord and *karka* increases the good effect of that house matters. The result is maximum when all the three factors are strong, and gets correspondingly reduced with two or one factor being strong.

As stated earlier, the planets are categorized as natural benefics (Jupiter, Venus, *Pakshabali* Moon and unafflicted Mercury), and natural malefics (Mars, Saturn, Rahu and Ketu). The Sun is regarded cruel. *Lagna* lord whether natural benefic or malefic is always favourable to the native. *Lagna* lord is also exempt from simultaneous ownership of *Trika* (6,8,12) houses. However, the functional nature of other planets undergoes change when the sign (*Rasi*) owned by these falls in a benefic or malefic (6,8,12) house of the horoscope.

When the *Mooltrikona* sign of a planet falls in *Trine* (5,9) house it is favourable. When a planet owns both a *Kendra* and *Trikona* it becomes *Yoga Karka* (most favourable). The benefic and malefic planets owning *Kendra* (4,7,10) houses do not give their natural result and act as neutral. The lord of 8th house is considered the most malefic.

These details are tabulated below for ready reference.

Functional Benefic and Malefic Planets for 12 *Lagna* with lordship.

Lagna	Benefic (favourable)	*Yogakarka* (Most favourable)	Neutral	Malefic (unfavourable)
1. Aires	Mars (1,8) Sun (5) Jup. (9,12)	-	Moon (4)	Venus (2,7) Mercury (3,6) Saturn (10, 11)
2. Taurus	Venus (1,6) Mercury (2,5)	Saturn (9,10)	Sun (4)	Moon (3) Mars (7,12) Jup. (8,11)
3. Gemini	Mercury (1,4) Venus (5,12) Saturn (8,9)	-	Moon (2)	Sun (3) Mars (6,11) Jup. (7,10)
4. Cancer	Moon (1) Jup. (6,9)	Mars (5,10)	Sun (2)	Merc. (3,12) Venus (4,11) Saturn (7,8)
5. Leo	Sun (1) Jup. (5,8)	Mars (4,9)	Merc. (2,11) Moon (12)	Venus (3,10) Sat. (6,7)
6. Virgo	Merc. (1,10) Venus (2,9)	-	Sat. (5,6) Moon (11)	Mars (3,8) Jup. (4,7) Sun (12)
7. Libra	Venus (1,8)	Saturn (4,5)	Moon (10) Merc. (9,12)	Jup. (3,6) Sun (11) Mars (2,7)
8. Scorpio	Mars (1,6) Moon (9) Jup. (2,5)	-	Sun (10)	Merc. (8,11) Venus (7,12) Sat. (3,4)
9. Sagittarius	Jup. (1,4) Mars (5,12) Sun (9)	-	Merc. (7,10)	Venus (6,11) Sat. (2,3) Moon (8)
10. Capricorn	Sat. (1,2) Merc. (6,9)	Venus (5,10)	Moon (7)	Mars (4,11) Jup. (3,12) Sun (8)
11. Aquarius	Sat. (1,12) Jup. (2,11)	Venus (4,9)	Mars (3,10) Sun (7) Merc. (5,8)	Moon (6)
12. Pisces	Jup. (1,10) Mars (2,9) Moon (5)	-	Sun (6) Merc. (4,7)	Venus (3,8) Sat. (10,11)

The above discussion clearly shows the close connection among signs, *bhavas* and planets for forecasting future.

Chapter VI

Nakshatras

'Nakshatra' is a Sanskrit word which is explained as 'न क्षरति न सरति इति नक्षत्र:।' meaning "That which is stable and static is *Nakshatra.*" Our ancient *Rishis* selected 27 (initially 28) clusters of fixed stars in the background of Zodiac for knowing the exact location of the planets in constant motion, and assess their effect on human beings. These *Nakshatras* are named after the major star in the cluster. The 360° oblong Zodiac starting from 0° *Mesha* (Aries) is divided into 27 *Nakshatras* of 13° 20' each from *Aswini* to *Revati*, and accommodates these into 12 *Rasis* (signs) of 30° each from Aries to Pisces. These 27 *Nakshatras* are equally allotted (3 each) among the 9 planets in a specific order in three cycles. Every sign contains two and a quarter *Nakshatra*, and each *Nakshatra* is further divided into four *charan* or *pada* (parts) of 3° 20'. Thus there are 9 *Nakshatra pada* in each sign. Each *Nakshatra pada* is allotted an alphabet which is used for naming the new born child, and facilitates knowing the birth *Nakshatra* of that individual in future. However, this is not strictly followed now. The effect of each *Nakshatra pada*, and the planets located therein are a subject of deeper astrological import.

Nakshatras have a fundamental role in timing of various events in an individual's life. When Moon at birth is located in any of the 27 *Nakshatras* it is called *Janma* (birth) *Nakshatra*. An individual starts his life with the *Dasa* of the lord of *Janma Nakshatra*. The duration of *Vimshottari dasa* of birth *Nakshatra* lord to be undergone is calculated, after which the *Dasas* of other planets follow in fixed order. In a *Dasa*, the *Bhukti* and *Antara* period also follow in the same sequence.

The lords of different *Nakshatras* and the duration of *Vimshottari dasa* of their lords are as under.

Planet	Nakshatra ruled (No.)	Dasa period
Ketu	(1) *Aswini*, (10) *Magha* and (19) *Mula*	7 Years
Venus	(2) *Bharani*, (11) *Purva Phalguni*, and (20) *Purva Shada*	20 Years
Sun	(3) *Kritika*, (12) *Uttara Phalguni* and (21) *Uttara Shada*	6 Years
Moon	(4) *Rohini*, (13) *Hasta* and (22) *Sravana*	10 Years
Mars	(5) *Mrigsira*, (14) *Chitra* and (23) *Dhanishta*	7 Years
Rahu	(6) *Aridra*, (15) *Swati* and (24) *Satabisha*	18 Years
Jupiter	(7) *Punarvasu*, (16) *Visakha* and (25) *Purvabhadra*	16 Years
Saturn	(8) *Pushya*, (17) *Anuradha* and (26) *Uttarabhadra*	19 Years
Mercury	(9) *Ashlesha*, (18) *Jyestha* and (27) *Revati*	17 Years

The 27 *Nakshatra* are considered auspicious or inauspicious with reference to *Janma Nakshatra* as follows.

Nakshatra	No. of Nakshatra	Quality
1. *Janma* (birth)	1, 10, 19	Inauspicious - For person's physical body.
2. *Sampat* (wealth)	2, 11, 20	Auspicious - For finance.
3. *Vipat* (Danger)	3, 12, 21	Inauspicious - Causes loss and accident.
4. *Kshem* (Welfare)	4, 13, 22	Auspicious - For prosperity.
5. *Pratyak* (Obstructive)	5, 14, 23	Inauspicious - Obstructive in progress.
6. *Sadhak* (Success)	6, 15, 24	Auspicious - For realization of ambition.
7. *Vadh or Nidhan* (Killer)	7, 16, 25	Inauspicious - Dangerous.
8. *Mitra* (Friend)	8, 17, 26	Auspicious - Favourable.
9. *Param Mitra* (Best Friend)	9, 18, 27	Auspicious - Very favourable.

This categorization is called '*Tarabala*'. *Janma, Vipat, Pratyek* and *Vadh Nakshatra* present on a day is avoided for all important undertakings like starting an enterprise, marriage and proceeding on important journey. *Janma Nakshatra* is least harmful.

Auspicious and inauspicious *Nakshatras* also influence the result of the planets located therein. Strong favourable planets in a horoscope are normally expected to give favourable result during their *Dasa-Bhukti* and transit. When the favourable planets are located in auspicious *Nakshatra*, the native enjoys very favourable result, but if favourable planet is posited in inauspicious *Nakshatra* then some bad effect will also be experienced. When unfavourable planets are posited in auspicious *Nakshatra*, the evil results get mellowed down. When unfavourable planets are located in inauspicious *Nakshatras* the malefic influence predominates.

The next importance of *Nakshatra* lies in imparting special strength to the planets located there. For example, the Sun represents *Atma* or soul. The final aim of human life in all the religions is to attain God and achieve liberation (*Moksha*). *Moksha* is signified by Ketu. When the Sun is in *Aswini* (Ketu) *Nakshatra*, it comes under the highest spiritual influence and is not influenced by the distracting characteristics of Aries sign and its lord Mars. The highest exaltation degree of the Sun is at 10° in Aries sign in Ketu *Nakshatra*. At exact opposite degree, i.e., 10° in Libra sign, the Sun is in deep debilitation.

Similarly, the exaltation points of other planets are fixed in appropriate *Nakshatra* and sign, where the planet displays its strength and quality in full measure. Thus *Nakshatras* play an important role by helping a planet attain maximum strength. The exaltation of planets with *Nakshatra* is tabulated below for ready reference:

Planet	Exaltation sign and degree	*Nakshatra* and its lord
Sun	Aries – 10°	*Aswini* (Ketu)
Moon	Taurus – 3°	*Kritika* (Sun)
Mars	Capricorn – 28°	*Dhanishta* (Mars)
Mercury	Virgo – 15°	*Hasta* (Moon)
Jupiter	Cancer – 5°	*Pushya* (Saturn)
Venus	Pisces – 27°	*Revati* (Mercury)
Saturn	Libra – 20°	*Swati* (Rahu)
Rahu	Gemini – 10°	*Aridra* (Rahu)
Ketu	Sagittarius – 10°	*Mula* (Ketu)

Note: The planets are in deep debilitation at 180° from exaltation point, i.e., in the opposite sign at the same degree.

There is similarity in the quality and nature of *Nakshatra* and their lord. The inherent traits of different planets, their *Nakshatras*, and their effect are tabulated for easy comprehension. These traits become prominent when the *Lagna* rises in respective *Nakshatra*.

Nakshatras

Planet	Nakshatras ruled	Inherent nature	Effect
Jupiter	*Punarvasu*, *Visakha* and *Purvabhadrapada*	*Satwik*	Purity of nature and inclined to do good.
Mercury	*Ashlesha*, *Jyestha* and *Revati*	-do-	-do-
Sun	*Kritika*, *Uttara Phalguni* and *Uttara Shada*	*Rajsik*	Mixed (both good and bad) result.
Moon	*Rohini*, *Hasta* and *Sravana*	-do-	-do-
Venus	*Bharani*, *Purva Phalguni* and *Purva Shada*	-do-	-do-
Mars	*Mrigsira*, *Chitra* and *Dhanishta*	*Tamsik*	Evil in nature.
Saturn	*Pushya*, *Anuradha* and *Uttarabhadrapada*	-do-	-do-
Rahu	*Aridra*, *Swati* and *Satabisha*	-do-	-do-
Ketu	*Aswini*, *Magha* and *Moola*	-do-	-do-

The friendly relationship among planets according to their *Gunas* or basic nature is as follows:

Planet	Nature	*Satwik* friend	*Rajsik* friend	*Tamsik* friend
Sun	*Rajsik*	Jupiter	Moon	Mars
Moon	*Rajsik*	Mercury	Sun	-
Mars	*Tamsik*	Jupiter	Sun, Moon	-
Jupiter	*Satwik*	-	Sun, Moon	Mars
Venus	*Rajsik*	Mercury	-	Saturn, Rahu
Saturn	*Tamsik*	Mercury	Venus	Rahu
Mercury	*Satwik*	-	Sun Venus	Rahu
Rahu	*Tamsik*	Mercury	Venus	Saturn
Ketu	*Tamsik*	Mercury	Venus	Saturn

The resultant effect due to location of planets in different *Nakshatras* is as under:

Nature of Planet	Located in *Nakshatra*	Resultant Effect
Satwik	*Satwik*	Very Good
Rajsik	*Rajsik*	Very Good
Tamsik	*Tamsik*	Good
Satwik	*Rajsik*	Good
Satwik	*Tamsik*	Mixed
Tamsik	*Satwik*	Mixed
Tamsik	*Rajsik*	Evil
Rajsik	*Tamsik*	Evil

Effect of *Nakshatra* on planet's *dasa*

Nakshatras play an important role in unfoldment of *dasa* result of a planet. A planet primarily gives the result of the lord of *Nakshatra* in which it is located. When a planet is pure in its *Guna* (basic nature) by being in similar *Nakshatra*, then a *Rajsik* planet gives best result in the first portion of its *Dasa*; a *Satwik* planet in 2nd portion of its *dasa*, while a *Tamsik* planet gives its effect in the 3rd portion of its *dasa*, depending upon benefic or malefic aspect on the planet.

When the *Nakshatra* lord is different from the planet under consideration, the *Nakshatra* lord also influences the result. Experience shows that the *dasa* of a planet does not give uniform result throughout its term. The *Nakshatra pada* in which the planet is posited is a useful guide in this respect. For example, if Jupiter is posited in *Pushya Nakshatra*, 1st *pada*, ruled by Saturn, then the first four years of Jupiter *dasa* will have the effect of Saturn and the remaining 12 years that of Jupiter. When Jupiter is in *Pushya* 4th *pada*, then the first 12 years will give Jupiter's result and the last 4 years will be influenced by Saturn. For exmple:

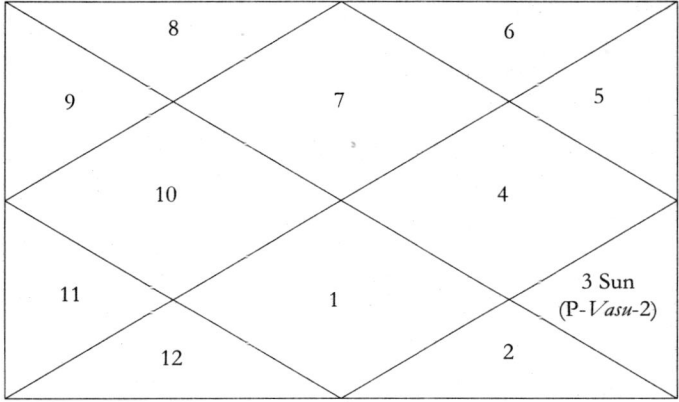

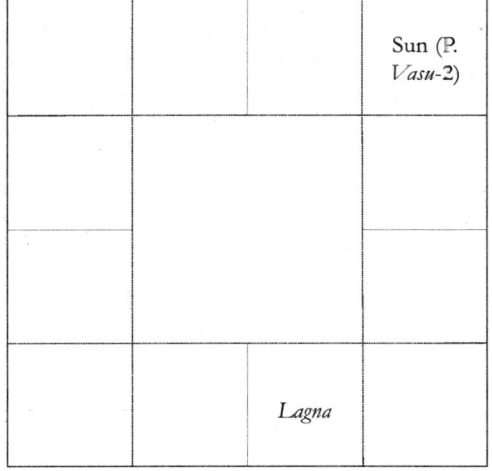

In this example horoscope of Libra *Lagna*, Sun, Lord of 11th house, posited in 9th house, should give good result in its *Dasa*. The Sun, a *Rajsik* planet, located in *Punarvasu*, a *Satwik Nakshatra* ruled by Jupiter, also points to good result. However, as Jupiter is the lord of 6th (an evil) house, it will cause illness or loss through theft as well. As Sun is posited in 2nd *pada* of *Punarvasu* ruled by Jupiter who is the lord of 3rd and 6th houses, the native will suffer illness or loss during the 2nd portion, i.e., between 1½ years to 3 years of Sun *Dasa*.

See another example,

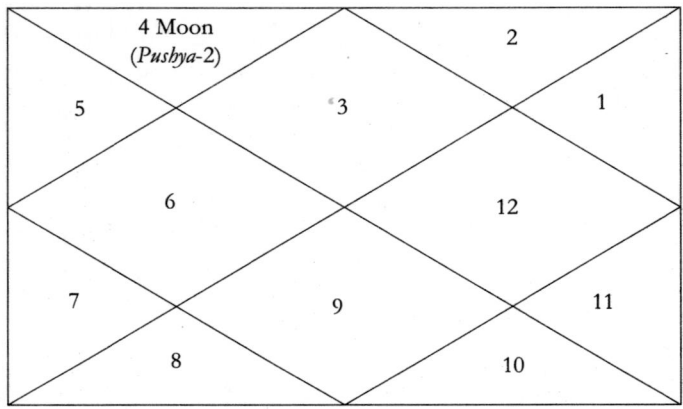

In this Gemini *Langa* horoscope, Moon lord of 2nd (wealth) is posited in its own sign Cancer, and should improve financial position of the person. But Moon is located in 2nd *pada* of *Pushya Nakshatra* Ruled by Saturn, who is lord of 8th and 9th houses. Hence, the native will suffer loss of wealth during 2nd portion (from 2 ½ to 5 years) of Moon *Dasa*. The result will also be influenced by benefic or malefic aspect on the Moon.

Nakshatra effect during Transit

The result of a planet transiting through certain *Nakshatra* also gets modified for better or worse. For example, during *Sade-sati* (7 ½ years transit of Saturn affecting Moon) when Saturn is in the sign of Cancer (for 2 ½ years) it will not cause much problem, as the *Nakshatras* in Cancer sign, i.e., *Punarvasu*, *Pushya* and *Ashlesha* are ruled by Jupiter, Saturn and Mercury respectively, which are cordial to Saturn. But Saturn's transit through Leo sign will be problematic during transit through *Magha* (Ketu) and *Uttara Phalguni* (Sun) *Nakshatra*.

Janma Nakshatra

As mentioned earlier, the *Nakshatra* where the Moon is posited at the time of individual's birth is called *Janma Nakshatra*. The 27 *Nakshatras* from *Janma Nakshatra* are divided into three groups of nine *Nakshatras* each. The first group consist of the nine *Nakshatras* beginning with the *Janma Nakshatra*; the second group starts with the 10th *Nakshatra*; and the third group with the 19th *Nakshatra*. The 3rd (*Vipat*), 5th (*Pratyak*), 7th (*Vadh*), 10th and 19th *Nakshatra* are prohibited in selection of day for starting an auspicious event like beginning of child education, solemnization of marriage, entry into a new house, starting of new business, or joining new post on transfer.

Janma Nakshatra in fact governs the whole life of the individual. It has direct influence on individual's social relations. His co-born, wife, partner, friends and other relatives born in the prohibited *Nakshatra* (3rd, 5th or 7th from *Janma Nakshatra*) will not prove sincere or will have inharmonious relation with the individual.

The transit of benefic planets, especially Jupiter and Venus, through *Janma Nakshatra* gives benefic result. Conversely, the transit of evil planets in *Janma Nakshatra* along with catalyst Rahu produce evil result, especially during *Nakshatra* lord *dasa*. Suppose an individual is born in *Kritika Nakshatra* then he starts his life with the balance of Sun *dasa* followed by the *Dasa* of Moon, Mars, Rahu, etc. To assess the result of any *Dasa* we have to carefully examine the benefic or malefic effect on *Janma Nakshatra* from time to time.

In this connection, a reference is made to the well known exposition in *Valmiki Ramayana* where King Dasharatha tells Shri Ram that his astrologers have cautioned that the King was heading for serious troubles as his *Janma Nakshatra Rohini* will be shortly afflicted by Mars, Sun and Rahu. This planetary configuration may give death like calamity or cause even his death. The king, therefore, decided to hand over the reigns of kingdom to his eldest prince Shri Ram. However, this could not materialize. The ensuing events led to King Dasharatha's death, while royal family and people faced serious problems. This historical fact indicates that even in that era the effect on *Janma Nakshatra* was studied while divining the future.

An examination of the above planetary affliction shows that Rahu is an arch enemy of Moon, the lord of *Rohini Nakshatra*. Rahu's conjunction with the Moon or the Sun causes *Grahana Yoga*. The combination of fiery Mars aggravated the situation. The combination of Saturn with Sun, Moon and Rahu in *Janma Nakshatra* creates slow and prolonged problems. The malefic effect is acute till Rahu transits through *Janma Nakshatra* (about 8 months and 11 days). The problems take serious turn during Rahu's transit through *Janma Nakshatra pada*. The eclipse of the Sun or Moon falling in *Janma Nakshatra* of any individual causes serious, and death like troubles to him.

Hence, whenever (i) the Sun or Moon is in proximity with Rahu in one's *Janma Nakshatra*, (ii) Mars and / or Saturn join them, or (iii) Mars, Saturn and Rahu flank *Janm Nakashatra* from both sides (causing *Papkartari Yoga*) the individual faces many problems in life. When Ketu, the counterpart of Rahu, transits through *Janma Nakshatra* (9 years after Rahu's transit), the native faces problems of somewhat lesser magnitude. One can look back into his life events and he will find that he had faced serious problems during the time his *Janma Nakshatra* was afflicted by Rahu and other malefic planets.

Thus, while divining the result of any *Dasa*, the good and bad effect of planets on *Janma Nakshatra* from time to time should invariably be taken note of.

Chapter VII

Varga Charts

A planet gives result commensurate with its strength or weakness in the horoscope. Two important methods mentioned in astrological classics for judging the strength of a planet are (i) its position in relevant *Varga (Divisional) Chart* – whether in exaltation, own or friendly sign and well aspected, and (ii) its standing in *Shadabala*.

Varga (Divisional) Charts

The *Lagna* Chart prepared for the date, time and place of birth of an individual shows the rising sign (*Lagna*) and planets in different houses, which indicate his physical and general well being in life. The 12 houses show different events in the life of that individual. Experience shows that on many occasions events which appear certain from *Lagna* Chart do not fructify exactly as anticipated, while some others occur which are not so prominent. The reason is not far to seek.

A *Rasi* (sign) consists of 30 degrees and a planet can be located therein anywhere between the first to 30th degree. Every degree of a sign has its own peculiarity and consequently a planet gives different result at different degree. Therefore, to correctly judge the nature of a planet's effect, the *Rasis* are divided into several parts. Our ancient *Rishis* have suggested many divisions which are called *Varga* or *Divisional Charts*. These vary from ½ division to $1/60^{th}$ division of a sign. The Divisional Charts are complementary to *Lagna* Chart and indicate the real potential of a planet to produce the result, and thereby help in correct and precise prediction. These charts may be termed as *'miniature horoscope'* for analyzing a specific event.

Maharishi Parasara, regarded as father of Indian Astrology, has referred to the following 16 Divisional Charts or *Shodasvargas*

Divisional Chart	Consulted for
1. *Lagna*	Body, appearance, general features and intrinsic strength.
2. *Hora* (½ sign Division)	Wealth and prosperity.
3. *Drekkana* (1/3 ")	Brother/Sister relationship, friends and nature of death.
4. *Chaturthamsa* (¼ ")	Happiness, property and success in competition.
5. *Saptamsa* (1/7 ")	Children and grand children.
6. *Navamsa* (1/9 ")	Marriage, spouse and planetary strength.
7. *Dasamsa* (1/10 ")	Career, profession and status.
8. *Dwadasamsa* (1/12 ")	Parental happiness.
9. *Shodasamsa* (1/16 ")	Conveyance.
10. *Vimsamsa* (1/20 ")	Religion and worship
11. *Chaturvimamsa* (1/24 ")	Educational attainment.
12. *Bhamsa* (1/26 ")	Strength and weakness.
13. *Trimasamsa* (1/30 ")	Tragedies and character of females
14. *Khavadamsa* (1/40 ")	These help in arriving at the
15. *Akshavedamsa* (1/45 ")	total strength of a planet in
16. *Shastiamsa* (1/60 ")	all the *Vargas*.

The Divisional Charts are referred to in brief as D-1 to D-60 respectively.

Acharya Verahamihir refers to only *Shadavargas* (Six Divisional Charts) namely, *Rasi, Hora, Drekkana, Navamsa, Dwadasamsa* and *Trimsamsa* (*Brihat Jatak*, 1.9). Acharya Kalidas in *Uttarakalamrita* (Ch. II, 3-4) refers to *Saptvarga* with the addition of *Saptamsa*. Acharya Manteswara in *Phaladeepika* (Ch.3) refers to *Dasavarga* (Ten Divisional) Charts – *Lagna, Hora, Drekkana, Saptamsa, Navamsa, Dasamsa, Dwadasamsa, Shodasamsa, Trimsamsa* and *Shastiamsa*. Most of the texts mention the manner of preparation of these *Varga Charts* without any further elaboration. The manually prepared horoscopes also did not mention *Varga Charts*, except *Navamsa*.

The astrological enquiries mainly relate to health, wealth, property, differences with co-borns, married life, progeny, profession/business, parents and serious tragedies, for which the *Lagna* Chart is examined along with *Hora, Drekkana, Saptamsa, Navamsa, Dasamsa, Dwadasamsa, Shodasamsa* or *Trimsamsa* Charts. These are discussed below.

Lagna Chart (D-1)

It is the basic chart. The physical and general well being of an individual is judged from *Lagna*. *Shastamsa* (D-6) Chart is also consulted for health purpose. Affliction to *Lagna* and its lord, and to *Shastamsa Lagna* and its lord indicates poor resistance against disease. When the current *dasa* lord is debilitated, in inimical sign or in 6th, 8th or 12th houses, or afflicted by malefics, the health of the individual suffers.

Hora Chart (D-2)

The *Hora* Chart is prepared by dividing the signs in two halves of 15° each. Each part is called a '*Hora*'. In odd signs, the first *Hora* (0° to 15°) is ruled by the Sun, and the second *Hora* (15° to 30°) is ruled by the Moon. In even signs this position is reversed, that is, 1st *Hora* is of Moon and 2nd *Hora* is of Sun. Moon *Hora* is numbered 4 (Cancer) and Sun *Hora* is numbered 5 (Leo).

The position of 2nd and 11th lords and *Karka* Jupiter in *Lagna* Chart is looked up in *Hora* Chart to judge wealth factor. *Chaturthamsa* (D-4) Chart is consulted to judge happiness and immovable property. *Ekadasamsa* (D-11) is examined for the possibility of sudden gains.

The *Hora* Chart *Lagna* is either in Sun *Hora* or in Moon *Hora*, and all the planets are located in these two *Horas*. An even sign in *Lagna* and Moon *Hora Lagna*, makes the native rich without much efforts. The native is good natured, contented and devoted to mother. When there is odd sign in *Lagna* and Sun *Hora Lagna* with Sun and other male planets (Jupiter and Mars) therein, the individual is bold and wealthy by own capability, effort and determination.

Male planets (Jupiter, Sun and Mars) in Sun *Hora*; female planets (Moon, Venus and Saturn) in Moon *Hora*, and Mercury in both *Hora* give good result. When Jupiter and Venus (*Karka* for wealth and prosperity) are in Sun *Hora Lagna* with Sun, the native enjoys wealth, status, respect and happiness. When Jupiter and Venus are in Moon Hora *Lagna* with Moon, the person is wealthy, happy and cultured. Benefics in Hora *Lagna* give good result while malefic planets give bad result.

Drekkana Chart (D-3)

Drekkana Chart is prepared by making 3 division of 10° each. The first *Drekkana* is ruled by the sign lord itself; the 2nd *Drekkana* is ruled by the 5th lord, and the 3rd *Drekkana* is ruled by the 9th lord. In a Fiery sign the 1st *Drekkana* is governed by its lord. The 2nd *Drekkana* by the lord of 5th sign, which is also Fiery sign, and the 3rd *Drekkana* is governed by the lord of 9th house, which is also a Fiery sign. This pattern is followed in Earthy, Airy and Watery signs as well. Acharya Varahamihir and Devajna Kalyan Verma have assigned a separate Chapter in their treatise *Brihat Jatak* and *Saravali* respectively, giving details about all the *Drekkanas*.

The *Drekkana* Chart indicates relationship with co borns. When lord of 3rd house in *Lagna* Chart is posited in friendly *Drekkana*, it indicates good result. A planet in own *Drekkana* confers virtues. When the Moon is posited in its own or in friendly *Drekkana*, the native is endowed with best qualities of body and mind. According to *Uttarkalamrita* the lord of *Lagna* occupying first, second or third *Drekkana* will make the native a judge, a ruler of *mandala* (district), or a head of the village, i.e., attain high status.

The *Drekkana* Chart is also used for knowing the nature of death. When the 22nd *Drekkana*, falling in the 8th house, is afflicted by malefics it causes death according to its nature. For example, *Ayuddha Drekkana* indicates death by injury, accident or gunfire; *Nigada Drekkana* indicates death by hanging, and *Sarpa Drekkana* indicates death by poison or suicide.

Chaturthamsa Chart (D-4)

This Chart is prepared by making 1/4th division of signs of 7° 30' each. The first part is ruled by the sign lord, the 2nd by the 4th lord, the 3rd by the 7th lord, and the 4th by the 10th lord.

This chart is studied for assessing comforts and immovable property to be enjoyed by the individual. The strength of 4th house lord and significator in *Lagna* Chart, the *Chaturthamsa Lagna* and 4th lord in that chart are also examined. When the *Lagna* lord and *Chaturthamsa* lord are friends, it ensures prosperity and happiness to the individual.

Saptamsa Chart (D-7)

This Chart is prepared by dividing the signs into 7 parts of 4° 17' 8" each. In odd signs, the *Saptamsa* divisions are ruled by the lords of 7 successive signs beginning with that sign itself. In even signs, these divisions are ruled by the lords of 7 successive signs beginning with 7th sign from that sign.

The *Saptamsa* Chart is examined to judge children, grand children and happiness from them. When *Saptamsa* Chart *Lagna* lord is a male planet, the native gets male progeny. When the lords of *Lagna* and *Saptamsa Lagna* are friends it indicates very favourable result. The 5th lord, planets in the 5th house, *Karka* Jupiter in *Lagna* Chart and *Saptamsa Lagna* and 5th house and its lord therein when strong confirm birth of male children and happiness from them. When these are weak or afflicted in *Saptamsa* Chart, the individual lacks happiness of progeny. A malefic planet in malefic *Rasi* in *Saptamsa Lagna* shows problems and unhappiness from children. When the *Saptamsa Lagna* lord is in 7th or 8th house conjoined with malefics the person lacks progeny.

A planet occupying its own *Saptamsa* bestows courage, wealth and fame.

Navamsa Chart (D-9)

Navamsa Chart is made on the basis of 1/9th divisions (of 3° 20' each) of the signs in *Lagna* Chart. In a Fiery sign, the 9 *Navamsa* divisons are ruled by the lord of the nine successive signs beginning with Aries. In Earthy signs, it is governed by the lords of 9 successive signs beginning with Capricorn. In Airy signs, the cycle begins with Libra, and in Watery sign with Cancer sign.

Navamsa Chart indicates marital happiness and characteristics of spouse. When *Navamsa Lagna* lord is benefic and in own *Rasi*, *Kendra* or *Trikona*, then the individual has happiness from marriage. When it is in 2nd or 11th house and strong, it gives wealth from marriage. If afflicted or located in 8th or 12th house the individual lacks marital happiness,

Another important use of *Navamsa* Chart is to judge the real potential of different planets in *Lagna* Chart. The position of 10th lord in *Lagna* and *Navamsa* Charts also indicates nature and success in profession.

A planet in same sign in *Lagna* and in *Navamsa* Chart becomes *Vargottam* and confers name, fame, success and prosperity. When *Lagna* and *Navamsa Lagna* lords are friends, the native enjoys marital happiness and comforts in life. Birth in *Vargottam Lagna* is considered fortunate.

The powerful *Yogas* found in *Lagna* Chart get diluted or neutralized when the planets forming the *Yogas* become weak or afflicated in *Navamsa*. If a planet is weak or afflicted in *Lagna* Chart but is well placed in *Navamsa*, then it gives good result.

Dasamsa Chart (D-10)

Dasamsa Chart is prepared on the basis of $1/10^{th}$ division (3° each) of signs in *Lagna* Chart. In odd signs, the *Dasamsa* are ruled by the lords of 10 successive signs starting with the sign itself. In an even sign, these are ruled by the lords of 10 successive signs beginning with the 9th sign from it.

This chart is examined to judge status, success and fame in profession. If the 10th lord and planets located in 10th house in *Lagna* Chart are strong in *Dasamsa* Chart, then the native enjoys success in his profession. When the planet in 10th house of *Lagna* Chart is located in a fixed sign in *Dasamsa* Chart and conjoins with a benefic planet, the native does business. But if that planet is in a movable sign and associated with malefic planet in *Dasamsa* Chart, then he does service. When a planet is good in *Lagna* Chart but weak in *Dasamsa* chart, the native achieves great success in his profession and then suffers a downfall. If *Lagna* lord and *Dasamsa Lagna* lord are friendly, the individual is successful in business, but when inimical then he suffers loss. For example, if Sun occupies the 10th house in *Lagna* Chart but occupies 12th house (loss) in *Dasamsa* Chart, the native rises in his profession followed by a downfall.

Dwadasamsa Chart (D-12)

This chart is made on the basis of $1/12^{th}$ division of signs (of 2° 30' each). In every sign, the *Dwadasamsa* portions are ruled by the lords of 12 successive signs beginning with the lord of that sign.

Dwadasamsa Chart is used to evaluate the parental help and happiness to be enjoyed by the individual. When the lord of *Dwadasamsa* Chart *Lagna* is male planet and is posited in own, friendly or exaltation sign and located in *Kendra* or *Trikona*, the individual gets full happiness of parents (father). When the *Dwadasamsa Lagna* lord is a female planet and located in similar position, the native enjoys more of maternal affection and happiness. If it is located in 6th, 8th or 12th houses, then such happiness is denied.

When the lord of *Lagna* Chart and lord of *Dwadasamsa Lagna* are friends, the native has good relations with parents. When the lord of 4th and 10th house in *Lagna* Chart are in friendly sign in *Dwadasamsa* Chart, the native gets full happiness and support of parents. Conversely, the result is otherwise. The conjunction of the Sun and Saturn creates enmity between father and son. Conjunction of Saturn and Moon creates differences between mother and son. The native becomes devout and helpful if a planet is in its own *Dwadasamsa*.

Shodasamsa Chart (D-16)

This Chart is formed on the basis of $1/16^{th}$ division of signs (of 1° 52' 30" each). In Movable signs, the *Shodasamsa* divisions are ruled by 16 successive signs beginning with Aries. In a Fixed sign, these are ruled by 16 successive signs beginning with Leo. In a Common sign, the reckoning is done from Sagittarius sign. This Chart is consulted for judging vehicular comforts of the native. The 4th house lord in *Lagna* and Venus strongly placed in *Shodasamsa* Chart ensures vehicle comfort in life.

Trimsamsa Chart (D-30)

This *Varga* Chart is prepared on the basis of 30 divisions of signs (of 1° each). In odd signs, the first 5 *Trimsamsa* are ruled by Mars, the next 5 by Saturn, the next 8 by Jupiter, the next 7 by Mercury and the last 5 are ruled by Venus. In even signs, the order is reversed, i.e., the first five *Trimsamsa* are ruled by Venus, the next 7 by Mercury, the next 8 by Jupiter, the next 5 by Saturn, and the last 5 by Mars. No *Trimsamsa* is assigned to Sun and Moon.

This chart is consulted to look up for tragedies and the character of a lady. A planet in own *Trimsamsa* gives good result. If planet indicates happiness in *Lagna* Chart but is weak or afflicted in *Trimsamsa* Chart, the native faces many difficulties in life during the *Dasa-Bhukti* of that planet, and its unfavourable transit fructify the event.

Judgment of *Varga* Charts

As will be evident from the foregoing, the preparation of *Varga* (Divisional) Charts requires much time and labour. This has now been made easy through computer programmes. These are now indicated in a computer generated horoscope for ready reference. For the preparation of these charts the birth time should be absolutely correct.

(1) A planet becomes very auspicious when it is located in exaltation, *Mooltrikona*, own or friendly sign, in *Kendra* or *Trikona* or *Vargottam* in many *Varga* Charts. However, a debilitated or combust planet in *Lagna* Chart even though strong in *Varga* Charts does not give expected result. A debilitated planet when *Vargottam* gives mixed result.

(2) When *Varga* Chart *Lagna* is aspected by benefic planets it enhances related result. For example, when *Navamsa Lagna* is

aspected by benefics, it is indicative of good comforts and marital happiness.

(3) When *Rasi* and *Varga* Chart *Lagnas* are identical then it gives very good result of the relevant matter, as if in *Vargottam*.

(4) Exchange of houses by planets in *Varga* Charts gives good result, provided it is not between evil house lords.

(5) A planet getting *Yogakarka* status in *Varga* Chart gives good result of the matter signified by it throughout life.

(6) The strength of *Rasi Lagna* lord should invariably be examined in *Varga* Charts. If it is in inimical divisions in many *Varga* Charts, the native suffers from poverty and struggles in life.

(7) When the lords of *Lagna*, *Navamsa Lagna* and *Drekkana Lagna* are strong, the native is blessed with every comfort in life and is very fortunate.

(8) A combust planet in *Lagna* Chart, when strong in some *Varga* Charts gives little good result.

(9) A planet in the 8th house in *Varga* Chart destroys the result indicated by it.

(10) When the 10th house and its lord is strong in *Lagna* Chart, *Navmsa*, *Dasamsa* and *Ekadasamsa* Charts, the native attains high status, and enjoys name and fame in that planet's *Dasa-Bhukti*.

(11) Moon in own *Drekkana* or friendly *Drekkana* makes the person handsome and attractive.

(12) A planet in own *Trimsamsa* gives good result.

Special Result of Varga Charts

When a planet is located in own, friendly, *Mooltrikona* or exaltation sign *in 2 Varga* Charts, it is called *Parijat* and confers noble qualities, wealth, recognition, happiness and prosperity.

When a planet is good in *3 Varga* Charts, it is a called *Uttam*, and makes the individual capable, wealthy, lucky, and popular.

When a planet occupies good position in *4 Varga* Charts it is called *Gopur*, and blesses the native with wisdom, wealth and property.

When a planet occupies benefic position in *5 Varga* Charts it is called *Simhasana*. As the name suggests, it bestows royal (State) favour and trust, and the native lives his life like a King.

When a planet occupies benefic position in *6 Varga* Charts it is called *Parvat*, and bestows the native sophisticated vehicles, and he leads an aristocratic life.

When a planet occupies good position in *7 Varga* Charts, it is called *Devaloka* and makes the native a popular ruler or administrator.

When a planet is good in *8 Varga* Charts, it is called *Suraloka*, and confers on the native good luck, wealth, progeny and high status.

When a planet is good in *9 Varga* Charts it is called *Airavata* and makes the native fabulous like God Indra on earth, who enjoys great wealth, name and fame.

When a planet is good in 10 *Varga* Charts it is called *Sridhama* or *Vaisheshik* and confers excellent luck, prosperity and wealth like a king.

In the chart below see the position of Jupiter:

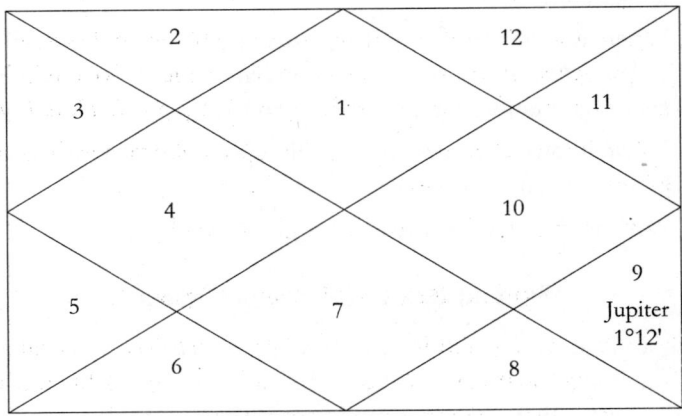

Varga Charts

	Lagna		
Jupiter 1°12'			

Here Jupiter is at 1° 12' in Sagittarius sign. Hence, it is in (i) own *Mooltrikona* sign in *Lagna* Chart, (ii) own *Drekkana*, (iii) own *Saptamsa*, (iv) own *Dasamsa*, (v) own *Dwasamsa*, and (vi) own *Shodasamsa*. By virtue of its occupying good position in six Divisional (*Varga*) Charts it attains *Parvatamsa* and confers a highly dignified life with comfort of excellent vehicles to the native in its *Dasa-Bhukti*.

Chapter VIII
Shadabala of Planets

A planet gives result commensurate with its strength or weakness in the horoscope. A benefic planet though well placed in birth chart will give very little result if it is weak. By virtue of its location in different houses of the horoscope, and aspect received, a planet gains or loses its inherent strength to produce its result. The strength of a planet unfolds itself in the form of actual result during its *Dasa-Bhukti*.

The sources of strength of planets are called *Shadbala*. As the name suggests, these refer to six (*Shada*) types of strength (*bala*). A planet strong in many *Shadabalas* gives very good result. The calculation of *Shadabalas* requires mathematical acumen and thorough knowledge of astrological principles. The intricate and elaborate procedure has now been made easy by computer programmes on astrology, which indicate comparative *Shadabalas* of the planets in the horoscope through vertical towers along with their numerical strength. *Shadabala* strength is measured in *Rupa* which is equal to 60 *Shastiamsas*. The actual strength of a planet is worked out proportionately.

The six-fold strength of planets is as follows.

(1) *Sthan Bala* (positional) - It comprises *Ucchabala, Saptvargabala, Kendrabala, Drekkanabala, Ojayugm Rasyamsa Bala*

(position in odd or even sign in *Rasi* and *Navamsa* Charts).

(2) *Kala Bala* (Temporal Strength) - It includes *Paksha*, (fortnights of Moon), *Varsha* (Year), *Masa*

Shadabala of Planets

			(month), *Din* (week day), *Hora* (hour), *Yuddha* and *Ayan balas*.
(3)	*Dig Bala* (Directional Strength)	-	Location of planets in favourable directions.
(4)	*Cheshta Bala*	-	Motional strength
(5)	*Drik Bala* (Aspectual Strength)	-	Effect of benefic or malefic aspect.
(6)	*Naisargika Bala* (Inherent Strength)	-	Inherent benefic or malefic strength.

In addition, the strength of a *Bhava* is assessed by *Bhavadipati Bala*, *Bhava Digbala* and *Drik Bala*. The strength of a *Bhava* is considered equal to that of its lord. A *Bhava* is strong when it is occupied or aspected by its lord, Jupiter, Venus or Mercury, and is not associated with or aspected by malefic planet.

Detailed Discussion

Sthan Bala

This is the most important and comprises many factors. When the planets are in *Kendra* (1, 4, 7, 10) *Panphara* (2, 5, 8, 11), *Apoklima* (3, 6, 9, 12) houses from *Lagna*, these get 1, ½ and ¼ *Rupa* strength respectively.

The strength of planets occupying the four *Kendras* is ¼ *Rupa* in 4th house, ½ *Rupa* in 10th house, ¾ *Rupa* in 7th house and one full *Rupa* in the first house or *Lagna*.

A planet becomes ineffective when located in *Bhava Sandhi*, whereas at *Bhava Madhya* it gives full result of the *Bhava* during its *Dasa-Bhukti*.

A planet in inimical sign, debilitation or *Asta* (Combust) also does not produce any worthwhile effect. The degrees of combustion of different planets from the Sun are – Moon 12°, Mars 17°, Mercury 14°, Jupiter 11°, Venus 10°, and Saturn 15°. These are in deep combustion within 5° from the Sun. Even though the planet be exalted, in own or friendly sign or *Navamsa*; it becomes ineffective when combust by the Sun.

The positional strength of the planet is full one *Rupa* if it occupies its exaltation sign. This strength is ¾ *Rupa* when the planet is in *Mooltrikona* sign. A *Vargottam* planet has strength like in *Mooltrikona*. A planet in conjunction with an exalted planet gets ½ *Rupa* strength. It is ½ *Rupa* when in own sign, and it is ¼ *Rupa* in friendly sign. In *neutral* sign, it is $1/8^{th}$ *Rupa*. In an inimical sign, the planet gets little *bala*. The strength is nil when it is debilitated or eclipsed by the Sun. It is $3/4^{th}$ *Rupa* in the sign of great friend (*Adhi Mitra* – both natural and temporary friend), and it is 1/32 *Rupa* in bitter enemy's sign (*Adhi-Shatru* – natural enemy and temporary enemy). A planet with positional strength gives perennial happiness, courage, stable mind, and independent profession.

The non-luminous planets are strong when these are in retrograde motion. Jupiter, Saturn and Mars become retrograde when these transit in 6th, 7th and 8th place from the Sun. The strength of a retrograde planet is equal to exaltation i.e., 1 *Rupa*. A planet conjoined with a Retrograde planet gets ½ *Rupa* strength.

Kalidas states in *Uttarakalamrita* (Ch.II.6) that an exalted but retrograde planet is like a debilitated planet and has no strength, while a retrograde planet in debilitation has the strength of exaltation. However, there is no unanimity on this view.

Kala Bala (Temporal strength)

Natural benefics are strong in the bright fortnight of Moon, whereas natural malefics are strong during the dark fortnight.

The Sun, Jupiter and Venus are strong during the day. Their strength is 1 *Rupa* at midday and nil at midnight.

Mercury is strong both during day and night and gets 1 *Rupa*.

Mars, Moon and Saturn are strong at night. Their strength is 1*Rupa* at midnight and nil at Noon.

When two planets are in the same house and within one degree, these are said to be at war (*Graha Yuddha*). The planet which is ahead of the other is the winner. The victorious planet gets 1 *Rupa* and the vanquished loses 1 *Rupa* in strength. Only the Sun and Moon do not enter into planetary war.

When planets are lord of the year, month, week day and hour, these get ¼ *Rupa*, ½ *Rupa*, ¾ *Rupa* and 1 *Rupa* strength respectively. Every planet is strong in its hour, day, month and year in descending order.

The Sun, Jupiter, Venus and Mars have *Ayanbala* in their Northern course (Capricorn to Gemini). Saturn and the Moon have *Ayanbala* during their Southern course (Cancer to Sagittarius). Mercury is always strong. A planet with *Ayanbala* takes the native to its direction and confers wealth and fame, provided it is not debilitated or *asta*.

Dig Bala

The planets get 1 *Rupa* strength as follows:
(1) Mercury and Jupiter in the East (*Lagna*).
(2) Venus and the Moon in the North (4th house).
(3) Saturn in the West (7th house), and
(4) The Sun and Mars in the South (10th house).

The *Digbala* is nil in opposite house where the planet has *Digbala*. In other places it is calculated proportionately.

A planet with directional strength takes the native to the direction ruled by it and confers wealth and happiness there, provided the planet is not combust or debilitated.

Cheshta Bala

The Moon has full *Cheshta Bala* at *Purnima* (full Moon). Planets with strong Moon attain *Cheshta Bala*.

The Sun gets *Cheshta Bala* when posited in Northern Course (*Uttarayana* – from Capricorn to Gemini).

Other planets (Venus, Mars, Mercury, Jupiter and Saturn) get full *Cheshta Bala* when these are in retrograde motion. Their *Cheshta Bala* is calculated from their mean position and *Shreegraha Kendra* through elaborate calculation.

A planet with *Cheshta Bala* intermittently gives money, fame and authority.

Drik Bala (aspectual strength)

The aspect of a benefic planet gives strength to the aspected planet, while the aspect of a malefic is detrimental. There is special full aspect for Jupiter, Mars and Saturn – on 5th and 9th; 4th and 8th; and 3rd and 10th signs, respectively besides usual 7th aspect. A planet gains strength when in conjunction with, or aspected by, a friendly or benefic planet. A planet becomes weak if it is in conjunction with, or aspected by, malefic planet.

Naisargika Bala (inherent strength)

All planets have inherent natural strength depending on their luminosity. The Sun has the greatest *Naisargika Bala*, while Saturn being the darkest planet has the least *Naisargika Bala*. The *Naisargika Bala* of planets is as follows:

Planet	Naisargika Bala	
Sun	60.00	*Shastiamsa* (1 *Rupa*)
Moon	51.43	"
Venus	42.05	"
Jupiter	34.28	"
Mercury	25.70	"
Mars	17.14	"
Saturn	8.57	"

The planets are considered strong in *Shadabala* when the Sun gets 6 ½ *Rupa*, *Moon* 6 *Rupa*, Mars 5 *Rupa*, Mercury 7 *Rupa*, Jupiter 6 ½ *Rupa*, Venus 5 ½ *Rupa* and Saturn 5 *Rupa*. A planet can have maximum 10 *Rupa* in *Shadabala*, when it is regarded the most strong and gives highly favourable result during its *Dasa-Bhukti*. A planet having less than 5 *Rupa* is considered weak. Among the several planets associated with a *Bhava*, that which has the greatest *Shadabala*, influences that *Bhava* the most.

Shadabala of Planets

A planet within first or last 6° of a sign is considered weak. The Moon in combustion gives malefic result. Other planets in combustion give mixed result of the Sun and their own, with the Sun dominating the combination.

If at birth, benefic planets possess good strength in *Shadabala*, the native has good habits, is truthful, upright and wealthy. On the other hand, should malefics be strong in *Shadabala* at birth the native will be a miser, indulge in bad deeds, is selfish and ungrateful.

Given below is the horoscope of a high ranking officer.

(1) Male, DOB: 17.8.1973, 6.12 A.M., Poona.

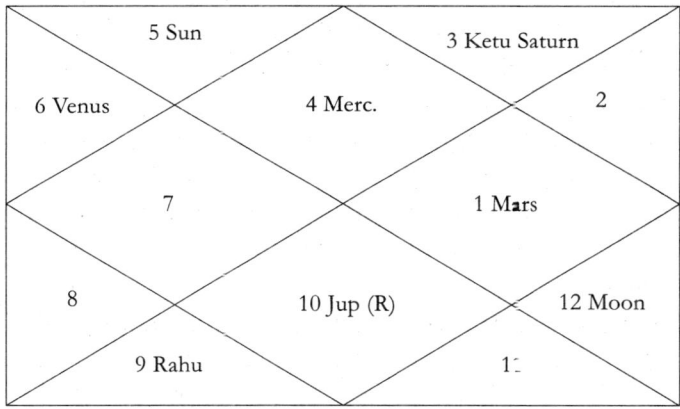

Moon	Mars		Ketu Saturn
			Lagna Merc
Jup. (R)			Sun
Rahu			Venus

Three *Kendras* in the horoscope are occupied by planets. The two salient features of the above horoscope are – first, the Sun which is in Leo sign in *Lagna* Chart is in own, friendly or exaltation sign in 9 *Varga* Charts and acquires *Airavatamsa*, and it has the highest *Shadabala* strength (8.72 *Rupa*), which makes the native highly placed in life and popular. The *Airavatamsa* position equates a person with Indra Deva on earth.

The other salient feature is that Mars, which is a *Yogakarka* for the horoscope, and placed in own sign in 10th house, has *Dig Bala*, forms *Ruchuk Panch Mahapurusha Yoga*, has the second best (8.31 *Rupa*) *shadabala* strength, and attains *Simhasana* in *Shadavarga*. Thus *Yoga karka* Mars posited in 10th house (*Karmsthan*) is very powerful. The Sun and Mars are also in trine to each other.

The native is now in the middle of Ketu *Dasa*. The Venus *Dasa* which has 7.62 *Rupa Shadabala* will also be good. The horoscope will peak during Sun *Dasa*. The native has been advised to propitiate Lord Shiva to improve *Lagna* lord Moon posited in the 9th house but receives the 10th aspect of Saturn posited in 12th house with Ketu.

(2) Male, DOB: 18.5.1837, 8.21 P.M., Pathri (Maharashtra).

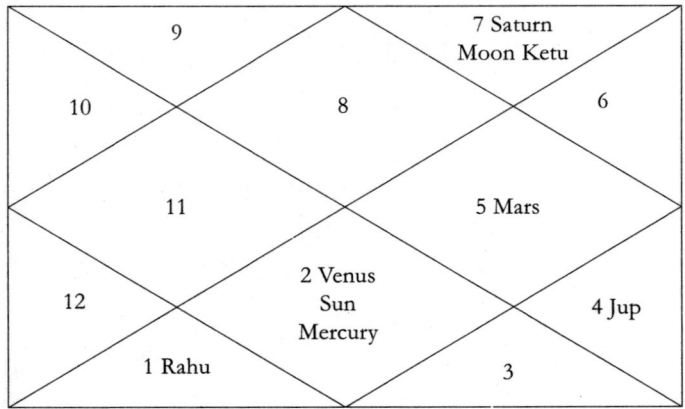

	Rahu	Venus Sun Mercury	
			Jup.
			Mars
	Lagna	Saturn Moon Ketu	

This is the horoscope of Shirdi Sai Baba. There is *Malavya Panch Mahapurusha Yoga* from *Lagna*, and *Hamsa* and *Sasa Pancha Mahapurusha Yoga* from Moon. There is also *Gajakesari Yoga* and *Saraswati Yoga* in the horoscope. *Lagna* lord Mars is very strong both in *Varga* Charts and *Shadabala*. Jupiter is next in strength in *Varga* Charts and *Shadabala*. Jupiter is lord of 5th house (*Purva punya*) and posited in 9th house (*Dharma*), and exalted there. Both Mars and Jupiter aspect *Lagna*. Jupiter, in turn, is aspected by exalted Saturn from 12th house. Saturn is conjoined with *Mokshakarka* Ketu and Moon. This planetary position made Sai Baba one of the greatest saints of India, whose fame is on the increase after shedding his mortal frame on 15.10.1918.

Chapter IX
Retrograde Planets

Our ancient *Rishis* were keen observers of planetary movement in the sky. They observed that nearer a planet is in its orbit to the Sun, the faster it moves, and the planets away from the Sun move at slow speed. They also noticed that from earth some planets appear to move forward upto a point, then stop moving further (become stationary) for a few days and thereafter start moving backwards (retrograde). After sometime these planets again become stationary for a few days, then start moving forward, reach the point from which these had retrograded and continue their forward motion in the Zodiac. This phenomenon repeats periodically. The *Rishis* also recorded the effect of every planetary movement on the human life and fortune of individuals and nations. Based on their experience they propounded some fundamental rules of astrology for the guidance of future generations. Modern Astronomical observatories equipped with sophisticated gadgets have corroborated the findings of our *Rishis*.

Our solar system consists of seven planets and two *Chhayagrahas* (Nodes). After the discovery of trans-Saturn planets, namely, Uranus, Neptune and Pluto, their effect on people and countries is being recorded. In the Ephemeris (showing daily planetary longitudes) published in English retrogression of a planet on a date is indicated by the alphabet 'R', and the date on which it turns direct by the alphabet 'D'. A planet is called 'Stationary' when there is no change in its longitude.

The Retrogression and Stationary period of different planets is as follow:

The Sun and the Moon are always in direct motion, while Rahu and Ketu always move in retrograde motion.

Mercury transits a sign in 25 days. It retrogrades approximately for 24 days on reaching a distance of 27° from the Sun. It retrogrades three times in a year, and is stationary for one day before and after retrogression.

Venus transits a sign in a month's time. It retrogrades when in the next sign to the Sun for approximately 45 days in alternate years. It is stationary for two days before and after retrogression.

Mars takes 45 days to transit a sign. When it reaches a distance of 135° from the Sun it becomes retrograde for approximately 80 days (sometimes longer). It may take upto 127 days to cover that sign and then covers the next sign in only 15 days in accelerated motion. It remains stationary for two to three days before and after retrogression.

Jupiter transits a sign in 12 to 13 months. It retrogrades approximately for 120 days in a year when in the 6th to 9th signs from the Sun. It remains stationary for five days before and after retrogression.

Saturn transits a sign in about 30 months, and retrogrades for approximately 140 days in a year, while transiting in 6th to 9th signs from the Sun. It remains stationary for about five days before and after retrogression.

Effect of Retrogression

Among the western astrologers, Allen Leo in '*Dictionary of Astrology*' observes, "This was once considered a sign of weakness and misfortune but it is doubtful whether there is any truth in the idea. Astrologers are much divided about it."

Edwin Raphael in his book '*The Key and Guide to Astrology*' states, "No planet is so strong beneficially when retrograde, as when direct or moving swiftly."

There is popular Western astrological saying, "When Jupiter retrogrades there is turn of future. When Saturn retrogrades relax a little."

Maharishi Parasara, father of Indian Astrology, mentions 8 types of planetary movements and their effect, including *Vakra Gati* (retrograde motion) (*Brihat Parasara Hora Shastra,* Ch. 28.). AcharyaVarahamihir states that *Vakra* (retrograde) planet gets *Cheshtabala* (special motional strength) (*Brihat Jatak,* Ch.2.20). His son Prithuyasas (*Horasara* Ch.3) states: "A retrograde planet is quite strong." Acharya Kalyana Verma states: "Benefics on becoming retrograde become very powerful and give kingly comforts to the individual in its *dasa.*" वक्रिणस्तु महावीर्या: शुभा राज्यप्रदा:। (*Saravali,* Ch.5.39). But the *dasa* of malefic retrograde planet causes grief and purposeless wandering.

Acharya Kalidas states in *Uttarakalamrita* (Ch.2.6) "A retrograde planet is strong like exalted planet and gets 1 *Rupa* strength. A planet conjoined with a retrograde planet also gets ½ *Rupa* strength". He adds "If an exalted planet in *Rasi* gets retrograde, it gives the result as if in debilitation, while a planet in debilitation and retrograde has the strength of exaltation." However, there is no unanimity on this point.

Acharya Manteswara states in *Phaladeepika* (Ch.4.2) "A planet not eclipsed by the rays of Sun, even if it is in debilitation *Rasi* or *Navamsa,* but retrograde, is very strong." (वक्रिणस्तु महावीर्या।) "A retrograde planet produces result as if occupying its exaltation sign." (वक्रगत: स्वोच्च फलं ।, *ibid,* IX.20).

Thus, all the authorities recognize the special effect of retrograde planets. A retrograde planet becomes powerful and produces notable results, depending on its lordship and occupation. If a planet is retrograde at birth it means that during this life until the planet completes its retrogression and turns direct, the person deals with things that have causes or beginning in his previous birth and still demand his attention.

Superior planets (Mars, Jupiter and Saturn) start slowing down on reaching 6th sign from the Sun. These are most retrograde in 7th and 8th sign from the Sun, and in the 9th sign these start their direct motion. Exact details can be obtained from Ephemeris.

Superior planets when retrograde are nearer to earth. Retrogression is maximum when these are in opposition to the Sun which makes these much brighter and their radiation reaches earth's surface in abundant measure like that of full Moon.

Inferior planets (Mercury and Venus) during retrogression remain between the Sun and earth with their darker side towards earth. As a result their radiation is very little and this increases their malefic tendency in proportion to their weakness. Many retrograde planets in birth chart indicate that success will be achieved after great effort.

Hence, special attention needs to be paid while interpreting the result of retrograde planets in a horoscope. This is discussed under the following heads: (i) Effect of retrograde planets in birth chart; (ii) Stationary planets during transit, (iii) Effect of planets turning retrograde during transit, and (iv) Effect of Retrogression on *Dasa* result.

PLANETS RETROGRADE IN BIRTH CHART

Mercury

When Mercury is retrograde in horoscope it makes the person hyperactive about the affairs of the house in which it is posited. The individual acts in haste and later on repents for his actions. The aspect of benefics on Mercury is helpful, while malefic aspect spoils it further.

Persons with Mercury retrograde in their horoscope are not practical and do not pay attention to facts and figures. They are successful in the realm of higher mathematics and deep philosophy. Their mind functions well on the abstract and sub-conscious level. Such individuals remain self-centred and do not seem to hear what others say to them. It is always worthwhile listening to them, though their talk may not be relevant to the matter in question. As astrologers they are more accurate in natal analysis than in predictive part.

When retrograde Mercury becomes direct in birth chart, there is marked change in the personality of the individual towards practicality. For example, if Mercury gets direct after 15 days from birth date, then (taking one day as one year) there will be positive change in the individual's personality and behaviour when he reaches 15th year, and the matters of the house of Mercury's location improve.

Venus

Venus is a female planet and is significator (*Karka*) for love, affection, emotions, sex and marriage. These features are disturbed when Venus is retrograde in the birth chart. Such individuals do not find enjoyment in things which most people consider pleasant, nor do they try to please others in the accepted ways. The individuals find it difficult to adjust in social conditions. Their idealistic image of love, sex and marriage are different from normal person. An element of self love predominates their personality.

With Venus retrograde in the birth chart, the individual tends to be fastidious about things others do not consider important, and is careless about things which are taken care by the majority. These persons incline towards unconventional expression of love. They may renounce physical love entirely, retreat into religious life, and become quite ritualistic. They have intense creative urge and succeed as artists, musicians, dancers, poets and dress designers. Their talent is, however, not recognized during their life time, but appreciated by next generation.

Venus represents woman in man's birth chart. A retrograde Venus in a man's horoscope can bring on manifold marital problems not attributable to any other factor. Venus can be retrograde for 45 days. If an individual is born when Venus started to slow down for retrogression, he may have Venus retrograde in his life for approximately 45 years, which would cover the normal span of married life. The effect of such Venus is usually disastrous for a happy married life. Retrograde Venus over emphasizes sex or nullifies it entirely. In case, it is afflicted by Mars, the native may become homosexual. Their wives may complain that after 4-5 years of marriage, their husbands seem to have lost love for them, and are running after other women. The husbands complain that the wife does not stimulate them as before.

Males born when Venus was retrograde for some weeks before their birth will find Venus turning direct approximately in their thirties. With direct movement of Venus in birth chart, the woman they were satisfied with during retrogression phase of Venus seems inadequate for them and they are inclined to seek other female partners. It makes little difference in which sign the retrograde Venus is located.

The degree of deviation in nature depends on the aspects received by Venus. The aspect of Saturn on retrograde Venus causes most troubles. The aspect of Mars inclines the native to use violent means to satisfy his desires.

Mars

Mars is a male planet and significator of vigour, energy and action. When Mars is retrograde in a male chart the physical energy and vitality of the individual do not rise to make him act. Such a person is like a spectator of cricket match, who has clear idea of what is going on in the ground but does not participate himself. These individuals are very good at planning and organizing physical activity by others, but detest own physical activity.

Like Venus, Mars is associated with the sex life of the individual. Mars is a male planet and represents a man in woman's chart. Mars and Venus are to be looked at first for sexual problems of an individual. Retrograde Mars in a woman's horoscope makes her frigid or over sexed. There seems to be no middle course.

Mars remains retrograde for approximately 60 to 80 days which represent sixty to eighty years of life. Before retrogression Mars moves in slow motion for about two weeks. The same happens when Mars becomes direct. During slow motion period it produces the same effect on the personality of women.

When Mars turns retrograde before birth its effect is more definite. The women may get married and have children without enjoying marital relations, and in some cases may even feel disgusted. Many such women complain that their husband have relationship with other women. When marital problems stem from sexual maladjustment, retrograde Mars in woman's chart may be the potent factor.

Jupiter

Jupiter covers a sign in 12 to 13 months. It remains retrograde for 120 days in a year. It remains stationary for 4 to 5 days before and after retrogression.

Individuals with retrograde Jupiter often find success in failure of others. They revive failing companies, uncover hidden assets, and are a bit surprised when the opportunities work out with ease. They are good in situations which involve an unknown element or chance factor. Jupiter retrograde in birth chart does not allow financial prosperity in life. Jupiter on turning direct in the natal chart makes the person successful and philanthropic.

Saturn

Saturn covers a sign in approximately 30 months. It remains retrograde for 140 days in a year, and remains stationary for about 5 days before and after retrogression.

Individuals with retrograde Saturn in their birth chart have a subconscious defeatism which underlines their most notable ambitions. They appear shy, introvert and lack in selfconfidence. They have a strong feeling that some unidentifiable force controls their destiny. They feel alone, isolated, separated from their fellow men and seldom understood. When Saturn turns direct in natal chart, the individual attains confidence and has taste of success.

Stationary planets

Before turning retrograde from direct motion, a planet slows down and remains stationary for a few days. Thereafter, before turning direct again remains stationary for a few days, turns direct, crosses the point from which it retrograded, and moves on.

When a planet becomes stationary on the radical position of a significator (*Karka*) its effect is very striking. Important events occur either before or after the time of its turning stationary. Stationary planets in transit are more powerful in their effect than when these are in direct motion.

Retrogression during Transit

Retrogression of a planet during transit produces significant change. When a planet is in retrogression it fails to give the result of the house (s) of which it is lord or significator. For example, when Jupiter is in retrogression that time is not good for one's finance, progeny, reputation and gains in general. If Jupiter happens to be the lord of 7th and 10th houses, the native's married life and working assignments will be adversely affected.

Notable recorded events show that the dates on which Mercury, Mars, Venus, Saturn and Jupiter in transit become stationary before retrogression or becoming direct has coincided with major events — good or bad - in individual and national affairs. Such events may relate to marriage, birth of son, gain in speculation or on the contrary, it may be about death, loss of power or authority. There is direct co-relation between the date of planet turning retrograde and the date of important events in the lives of individuals and national affairs. In many cases the incidents exactly coincide with the date planets change their course in transit, while in others the dates of incidents may either advance or fall back by some days. These periods usually coincide with the termination of on going action, or life itself, or the beginning of an activity which alters the status.

When a natural benefic while transitting a favourable house turns retrograde, it intensifies the good result. If the transited house be malefic the evil result will be reduced to the minimum.

On the contrary when a natural malefic transiting a favourable house turns retrograde it neutralizes the benefic result of transit, whereas retrogression in an unfavourable house increases malefic result. Retrogression of malefics in transit slows down and delays their natural effect. One should not make any important move until the malefic attains direct motion. When it turns direct again, the time is ripe for acting upon the plan for reaping the harvest.

Mercury

When Mercury turns retrograde, the person is likely to be indecisive. This is the time to slow down activities and stick to the routine. One should postpone changes in commitments, especially where contracts and agreements are concerned, until after Mercury is in direct motion. Events begun under retrograde Mercury terminate midway unsuccessfully or do not produce the desired result. Agreements signed when Mercury is retrograde seldom succeed, and changes made do not work out as expected. A short wait enables moving ahead faster later. There is an old adage, "Never begin anything new under retrograde Mercury, or delay and trouble occur."

Venus

When Venus turns retrograde in transit, it increases sexual urge in males and females, resulting in misplaced interest in opposite sex among adolescents. Malefic aspect on such Venus induces sex crimes. While wives expect extra love and care from their husbands, the husbands not getting reciprocal response from their wives turn to other ladies and indulge in excessive drinking. Such behaviour normalizes when Venus turns direct.

Mars

Mars turning retrograde in transit causes sudden excitement, fighting, rash actions, accident and aberrations in sex and marriage for which the native repents later. Physical vigour and energy is misdirected and its aspect on 6th, 8th or 12th houses and their lords causes accidents. It is observed that when Mars turns retrograde, or is in accelerated motion, the period of menstruation in ladies lasts a few days more than normal.

Jupiter

When Jupiter becomes stationary and turns retrograde it delays or withdraws opportunity, while a stationary-direct Jupiter gives success and restores the progress and benefits. Generally, people become worried about family, religion and duties when Jupiter turns retrograde in transit. When Jupiter is retrograde in the 2nd (wealth) house it is time to recover debts, go over past accounts, and make application for any dues or tax refund. When Jupiter is direct again in this house, it is time to go all out on new financial ventures. Retrograde Jupiter in 12th house causes difficulties in making things happen. A retrograde Jupiter in transit plays high drama in the life of political leaders than retrograde Saturn as is generally believed.

Saturn

When Saturn turns retrograde in a sign or in relation to a planet in birth chart, the native feels the pressure going away and he feels some respite. Retrograde motion of Saturn allows some time to review the situation. It is not complete respite, because on Saturn getting direct the native again feels the pressure. The period is best utilized to see what method, technique and efforts could be better employed to face the situation in hand.

When retrograde Saturn in transit aspects a planet which is retrograde at birth, the individual undergoes through enormous turmoil within, which he cannot explain to others.

When Saturn and Mars are retrograde in 10th house, or aspect it in a political leader's horoscope his fall from power becomes imminent, unless Jupiter or Venus act as saviour through benefic aspects.

Planets traversing Retrograde Space on turning Direct

When a retrograde planet turns direct and traverses back through the part of the Zodiac it transited earlier, there is an eleventh hour opportunity for gaining advantage and benefit.

Special Comments on Moon

Though Moon is never retrograde, the astrological savants are unanimous in holding not to start anything new or important on the day before new Moon (*Amavasya*). Similarly, one should not begin any undertaking when Moon is in a sign occupied by retrograde planet, because it will soon be adversely affected by Retrograde planet.

Effect of retrogression on *Dasa* Result

Dasa result are felt in ample measure when the planet in birth chart transitting through benefic house and sign of its strength remains in retrograde motion.

The *Dasa* of a planet retrograde in birth chart gives better result when it moves in direct motion.

When the planet retrograde in birth chart become retrograde in transit it becomes overactive and gives only mediocre result.

Example Horoscope

The effect of retrograde planets is amply evident in the horoscope of Mahatma Gandhi discussed below.

DOB: 2.10.1869, 8.25 A.M., Porbandar.

```
             8 Saturn           6 Sun
       9    7 Mercury            5
            Venus Mars
            10 Ketu           4 Moon
                              Rahu
      11    1 Jupiter            3
               (R)
              12                 2
```

	Jup (R)		
			Rahu Moon
Ketu			
	Sat.	Lagna Merc. Venus Mars	Sun

Retrograde Planets

Gandhi Ji intensified the independence struggle with the start of Jupiter (R) *Dasa* in 1940, and India attained Independence on 15th August, 1947. Both the *Dasa* lord Jupiter and *Bhukti* lord Venus got afflicted by transit Rahu-Ketu (in 7th and 1st house) from January, 1948.

Dasa lord Jupiter is posited in 7th (*Marka*) house. It is aspected by *Marka* Mars from *Lagna*. Mars is conjoined with *Lagna* and *Bhukti* lord Venus, and 12th lord Mercury. *Lagna* is in *Pap kartari Yoga*.

During the middle part of 3rd *Sade-sati*, Saturn became retrograde at 29° 32' in Cancer sign on 4th December, 1947 while transitting over natal Moon and Rahu in 10th house. It cast 3rd aspect on natal Sun in 12th house, 7th aspect on natal Ketu in 4th house, and 10th aspect on *Dasa* lord Jupiter in 7th house.

Transit Mars became retrograde in 11th house (Leo) on 8.1.1948, and cast 4th aspect on natal Saturn, with transit *Dasa* lord Jupiter, in 2nd house, and also afflicted *Lagna* lord and *Bhukti* lord Venus transiting through Aquarius (5th house).

The affliction of *Dasa* and *Bhukti* lords by transit Rahu-Ketu axis, and by retrograde Mars and Saturn of houses 2, 4, 5, 6, 7 and 12 in natal chart, gave much mental agony to Gandhi Ji due to unabated socio-political turmoil despite his fasts and repeated appeals for peace, and he fell to assassin's bullet on 30.1.1948.

On the fateful day transit Moon conjoined Sun in 12th house, received aspect of retrograde transit Saturn and was in *Pap kartari Yoga* formed by transit Ketu and Mars.

Chapter X

Important Planetary Yogas

'*Yoga*' is a special feature of Indian Astrology. The word '*Yoga*' (योग) has its root in Sanskrit word '*युग*' (*Yug*), which means 'link' or 'connection'. In Astrology it means inter-connection of planets. *Yoga* involves minimum two planets, except in the case of *Pancha Mahapurusha Yoga* wherein a single planet (Mars, Jupiter, Venus, Mercury or Saturn) occupying a *Kendra* (angle) indentical with its own or exaltation sign produces good result. Strong and well placed planets produce good result during their *Dasa-Bhukti*. Even one single planet in its highest exaltation, aspected by friendly planet in a person's horoscope gives him high status, prosperity and fame in its *Dasa-Bhukti*.

'*Yoga*' boosts up the strength of participating planets which produce benefic result for the native. Strong benefic planets forming *Yoga* in a good house (other than 6th, 8th, 12th) produce best result. But the *Yoga* formed by the lords of 6th, 8th or 12th houses with benefic planets produce evil result. However, when the lords of 6th, 8th and 12th houses become mutually related by conjunction or mutual aspect in these very houses, or exchange houses, and do not have relation with other planets, such *Yoga* makes the the native famous and prosperous during *Yoga* forming planets' *Dasa*. This is called *Vipreet Raj Yoga*.

One born with benefic *Yogas* leads a happy and prosperous life. Malefic *Yogas* produce inauspicious result, and the native faces many problems in life. There are hundreds of *Yogas* mentioned in Astrological classics from which the most important and useful ones are discussed here.

Formation of Yoga

According to Maharishi Parasara, the planets form *Yoga* in one of the following ways:

(1) The planets are located in each other's sign, i.e., inter-change their sign, such as the Sun be in Aries and Mars in Leo. This is also known as *Parivartana Yoga*. (*The best*).

(2) All the planets aspect the opposite sign, which is 7th aspect, while Jupiter, Saturn and Mars in addition have special aspects as well. The example of mutual aspect is Moon in Gemini and the Sun placed in 7th sign Sagittarius, and aspect each other (*2nd best*).

(3) One planet may cast full aspect on the other, but the latter does not aspect the former, such as Mars in Leo has 8th full aspect on the Sun in Pisces, but the Sun in Pisces does not aspect Mars in Leo (*3rd best*).

(4) The Planets are conjoined in a sign (*the last*).

Depending on their resultant effect these *Yogas* are called *Raj Yoga*, as erstwhile kings (*Rajas*) enjoyed these comforts. Strong *Raj Yogas* are present in the horoscope of Ministers and high ranking officers in present time. The *Yogas* conferring much wealth are called *Dhana Yogas*; those causing poverty and debt are called *Daridra Yoga*, and the *Yogas* causing problems and ill-health are called *Arishta Yoga*. There are some special *Yogas* as well.

In a horoscope, *Kendras* and *Trikonas* are regarded benefic houses and their lords give good result, with the condition that the benefics and malefics as lord of *Kendras* do not produce their actual result and behave as neutral. The *Trikona* lords always give good result. The 2nd house relates to wealth and 11th house to gains. The 9th house (*Bhagya*) is 5th from 5th (*Purva punya*), and the 5th from 9th house is *Lagna*. The *Lagna* is regarded both a *Kendra* and *Trikona* and its lord always produces good result. Planets in own, *Mooltrikona*, *Vargottam* and exaltation sign progressively give better result. For some *Lagnas*, when a single planet owns both a *Kendra* and a *Trikona* house, it becomes *Yoga karka*, or the most benefic planet for that *Lagna*, and gives excellent result in its *Dasa-Bhukti*. For example, Saturn is *Yoga karka* for Taurus and Libra *Lagna*, and Mars becomes *Yoga karka* for Cancer and Leo *Lagnas*. A *Yoga karka* planet having connection with another *Kendra*, *Trikona*, 2nd or 11th house lord produces excellent result.

The result of any *Yoga* depends on the nature, location and strength of the planets forming it. Planets forming *Yoga* give the best result when these are strong (exalted, in *Mooltrikona*, or own sign, and in similar location in *Navamsa*), the *Yoga* is formed in benefic house (other than 6, 8, or 12), and are aspected by benefics.

According to *Uttarakalamrita*, the planets may form a good or bad *Yoga* when they are within an orb of 12 degrees. Of these two, if the planet that has a slower average motion is in advance and one that has a faster average motion is behind, the *Yoga* yields good result. The *Yoga* result is fully realized when the planets are within one degree. The *Yoga* result becomes 'nil' when the planets are separated by 12°. In the intermediate position, the strength of the *Yoga* is judged proportionately. When the faster moving planet is already ahead by 12° or more, effect of the *Yoga* is not experienced by the native.

The *Yoga* results are to be interpreted keeping in view native's family and social background. The Astrological classics stipulate that a planetary *Yoga* which makes the son of a King also a King, it makes the son of any other person wealthy. (योगो यत्र नृप्पाजातो राजा तत्रन्यजो धनी।)

Before discussing particular *Yogas*, it is worthwhile to look up three important centres of a horoscope, known as 'Tripod' of the horoscope. These are *Lagna*, Moon sign, Sun sign and their lords. Sun represents 'self' and Moon refers to 'mind'. (आत्मा रवि शीतकरो मनस्तु।). Kalidas in *Uttarakalamrita* regards the *Lagna* as symbol of life's vital force, and the sign occupied by the Moon as body of the native. (लग्न प्राणमयं शशिस्थ भवनं देहस्तयोस्ततफलं।) Strong *Lagna*, Moon *Rasi* and Sun *Rasi* and their lords confer health, wealth, status and fame to the native.

Lagna and its Lord

Lagna is the pivot of an individual's horoscope. It indicates in brief, native's personality, temperament, health, status, prosperity, success and failures in life. All the Astrological classics lay emphasis on the strength of *Lagna* and its lord for enjoying a healthy, wealthy, prosperous and successful life. According to *Phaladeepika* (Ch. VI, 45) "When *Lagna* is occupied or aspected by benefics, and *Lagna* lord is exalted, or in own sign or a benefic house, it is called *Chamar Yoga*." Such an individual remains happy, healthy, prosperous and famous in his life.

On the contrary, "When the *Lagna* is associated with or aspected by a malefic, and the *Lagna* lord is weak and posited in a malefic place, it is called *Avayoga*." (*ibid*, Ch. VI, 68). A person born with *Avayoga* suffers from poverty, has bad character, suffers humiliation, associated with wicked people and is short lived.

When *Lagna* lord, whether natural benefic or malefic occupies or aspects the *Lagna*, it confers happiness, wealth and prominence. If *Lagna* is not owned by the aspecting planet, then the aspect of a benefic planet gives benefic result, and the aspect of a malefic planet produces evil result.

Birth in *Vargottam Lagna* is considered lucky. Good *Yogas* in the horoscope are effective when the *Lagna* and its lord are strong. The strength of *Lagna* is equal to that of its lord.

When the 2nd and 12th houses from *Lagna* are occupied by benefic planets, it is called *Shubha kartari Yoga*, and makes *Lagna* strong. It makes the individual healthy, happy, rich, and gives long life. But when *Lagna* is sandwitched between malefics, it is called *Pap kartari Yoga*, and weakens *Lagna*. Such an individual is poor, miserable, sick and has short life, if there is no benefic aspect on *Lagna* and *Lagna* lord. When benefic planets unaspected by malefics, occupy 2nd house from *Lagna*, the *Yoga* formed is called *Sasubha* and gives benefic result. The individual is gentle, wealthy and happy in life. Mixed planetary position produces mixed result.

According to *Sarvartha Chintamani*, "If the sign in *Lagna* belongs to a benefic planet, and it is also aspected by a benefic, the native gets comforts in life from early childhood. This is not so if the *Lagna* is associated with, and aspected by, a malefic. When the *Lagna* is associated with many malefic planets, the native faces trouble throughout life." (Ch. II, 94).

Saravali states:

केन्द्रे विलग्ननाथ: सुहृद्भिरभिवीक्षितो विहगै:।
लग्नस्थिते च सौम्ये भूपतिरिह जायते पुरूष:॥

(Ch. 35.38)

meaning, "The native will be a ruler (have high status) if the *Lagna* lord is in *Kendra* (angle) aspected by a friendly planet, while the *Lagna* is tenanted by a benefic."

Summarising the result of strong *Lagna* lord *Phaladeepika* (Ch.XX.2) states: "When the *Lagna* lord possesses maximum power, the native during its *Dasa* rises to eminence and is happily placed in life. He is physically strong and possesses a charming personality. His prosperity increases like that of the waxing (increasing) Moon."

On the other hand, "When *Lagna* lord is weak or afflicted the native during its *Dasa* will be imprisoned, lead an insignificant life, suffer from fear, diseases and mental anxiety, participate in funeral rites, suffer loss of position and other misfortunes." (*ibid*, Ch.XX.15)

(1) Swami Vivekananda,

   DOB: 12.1.1863, 6.20 AM, Calcutta.

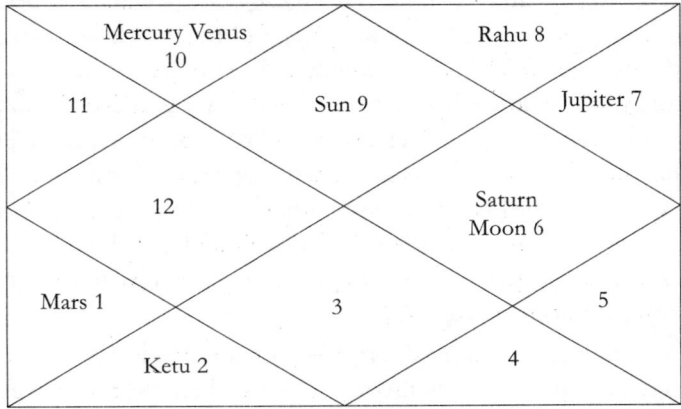

Important Planetary Yogas

	Mars	Ketu	
Merc. Venus			
Lagna Sun	Rahu	Jupiter	Saturn Moon

Lagna is *Vargottam*. The 9th lord Sun located in *Lagna* is also *Vargottam*. *Lagna* lord Jupiter is posited in 11th house and aspected by 5th lord Mars from 5th house. Thus *Lagna* is very strong. He had a strong body and majestic personality. The 10th lord Mercury and 11th lord Venus are conjoined in 2nd house. There is exchange between the 2nd house lord Saturn and the 10th house lord Mercury. This made him an excellent orator and he propagated Hindu religion abroad.

(2) Male, DOB: 18-4-1904, 6-05 AM, Kashipur (W.B.).

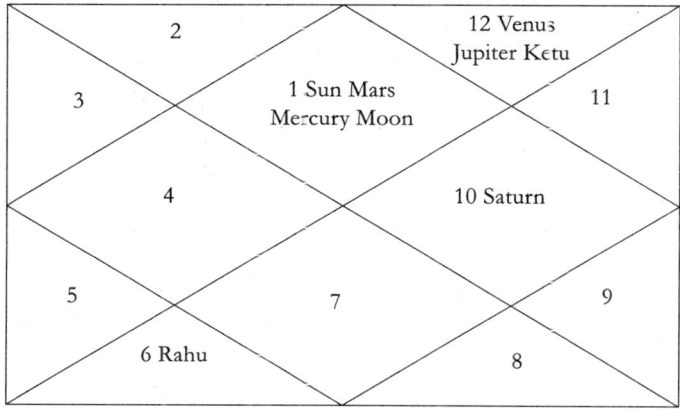

Venus Jup. Ketu	*Lagna* Sun Mars Merc. Moon		
Sat.			
			Rahu

Lagna lord Mars is in Aries *Lagna* and forms *Ruchuka Yoga*. Mars is conjoined with 4th lord Moon and 5th lord Sun. The Sun is also exalted. *Lagna* receives the support of *Karak* planet Saturn in 10th house in own sign and also forms *Sasa Yoga*. Venus, lord of 2nd and 7th houses, is exalted in 12th house, with 9th and 12th houses lord Jupiter and Ketu. These boost *Lagna*, *Lagna* lord and other planets located there, besides giving a religious and humanitarian approach. The horoscope belongs to an industrialist.

In contrast, see the following horoscope.

Male, DOB: 10.8.1970, 2.05 PM, Kharagpur.

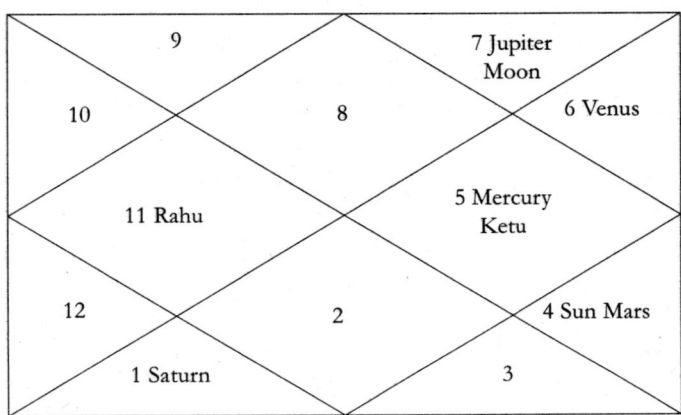

	Saturn		
Rahu			Sun Mars
			Mercury Ketu
	Lagna	Jupiter Moon	Venus

Lagna lord Mars is debilitated and combust. Lord of 2nd and 5th houses Jupiter is in 12th house, and afflicted by Rahu and Saturn. The 7th lord Venus is debilitated in 11th house (gains). As a result the native runs a small cloth shop and is leading an ordinary life. The *Gajakesari Yoga* formed in 12th house could not help him rise in life.

Lagnadhi Yoga

When benefics are posited in 6th, 7th and 8th houses from *Lagna*, free from aspect or company of malefics, these form *Lagnadhi Yoga*. The planets may be posited in one, two or in all the three houses. Such a person enjoys high status, is virtuous, wealthy, and lives long.

Female, DOB: 5.5.1963, 4.40 P.M., Amritsar.

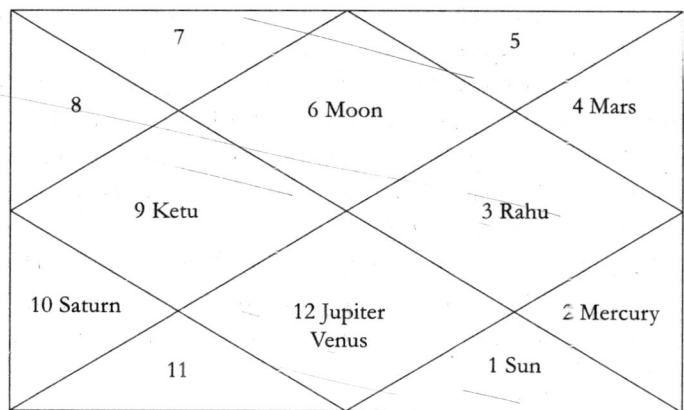

Jup. Venus	Sun	Merc.	Rahu
			Mars
Sat.			
Ketu			*Lagna* Moon

Both *Lagna* and Moon are in Virgo sign. The *Lagna*, Moon and Venus being in even sign have made her very beautiful and cultured. The 7th lord Jupiter and 9th lord Venus are conjoined in 7th house and aspected by strong Moon. There is sufficiently strong *Lagnadhi Yoga*, *Chandradhi Yoga* and *Laxmi Yoga*. *Lagna* lord Mercury is in 9th house. Jupiter forms *Hamsa* and *Gajakesari Yoga*, and Venus forms *Malavya Yoga*. The lady is the wife of a royal personage, extremely rich, endowed with fine qualities and dear to her husband.

Importance of Moon

Moon is chief significator of mind, mother, happiness, wealth and chest/lungs. All the classics recommend that analysis of a horoscope should be done from *Lagna* or Moon sign, whichever is stronger. Strength of Moon lies in its *Pakshabala* (पक्षोद्भवं हिमकरस्य विशिष्टमाहु:।) It has maximum strength on *Purnima* (full Moon). During night birth the location of Moon in 11th house removes many deficiencies in the horoscope. According to *Phaladeepika*, the strength of Moon gives strength to all other planets (चान्द्रं बलं तु निखिल ग्रहवीर्य बीजम्।) A planet conjoined with strong Moon gains in strength. Moon in deep debilitation (3° Scorpio) makes other good *Yogas* in the horoscope ineffective.

In addition:

(1) When *Pakshbali* Moon is aspected by a benefic planet, even a low born person becomes prosperous and famous like a King. The term 'King' should be understood as high personage in modern era.

(2) When the full Moon is in exaltation, the native will become generous and praiseworthy like a King.

(3) When full Moon occupies an angle other than the *Lagna*, the native will be like a King endowed with wealth, conveyances and authority.

(4) When full Moon occupies an *Upachaya* house (3, 6, 10, 11) and receives aspect from Jupiter, while the lord of the Moon sign occupies the 10th or 7th house, the native will become a ruler.

(5) When full Moon is exalted and *Vargottam*, and also aspected by a benefic planet, the person will become a famous ruler in the *Dasa* of that benefic planet, provided there is no strong malefic in *Kendra* from Moon.

(6) When the Moon is *Vargottam*, or in Cancer *Navamsa*, and aspected by a strong benefic, while the *Lagna* is free from malefic occupation, the native will become a powerful ruler endowed with physical splendour.

(7) When Moon is in *Kendra* (other than *Lagna*) or *Trikona*, and aspected by Jupiter and strong Venus, the native will be equal to a King.

Chandra Yogas

When in a horoscope the 12th house from Moon is occupied by a planet other than the Sun, Rahu and Ketu, the *Yoga* so formed is called '*Anfa*'. If there is a planet other than these planets in the 2nd house from Moon, the *yoga* formed is called '*Sunfa*'. When the 2nd and 12th houses from Moon are occupied by planets other than the Sun, Rahu and Ketu, the *Yoga* so formed is called '*Durudhara*'. The individual born with these *Yogas* is wise, moral, rich and leads a happy life. The actual result will depend on the nature and strength of the planets forming these *Yogas*. The Moon should also be *Pakshbali* (strong).

When there is no planet is the 2nd and the 12th house from Moon, the *Yoga* formed is called '*Kemadruma*'. It is a malefic *Yoga* and makes the native poor and restless. He suffers from diseases, faces troubles and wanders away from home. However, when the Moon is conjoined with a benefic planet, or when the Moon is in an angle, or when the Moon is full, or has planets in *Kendra* from it then *Kemadruma Yoga* becomes ineffective.

OTHER IMPORTANT *YOGAS*

(1) *Gajakesari Yoga*

The Moon in *Kendra* (angular) position from Jupiter forms *Gajakesari Yoga*. It makes a person wise, virtuous, famous, and he enjoys high status and long life. This *Yoga* gives good result in Cancer, Scorpio and Pisces *Lagna*; moderate result in Aries, Gemini, Virgo and Aquarius *Lagna*; and little good result in Taurus, Leo, Libra, Sagittarius and Capricorn *Lagna*.

Male, DOB: 30. 12. 1979, 10.40 A.M., Sasaram (Bihar).

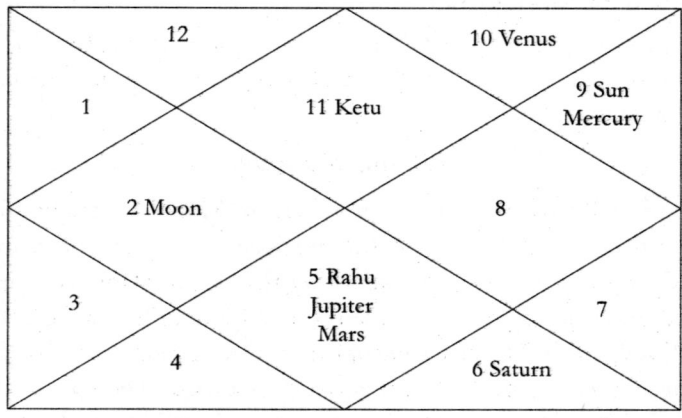

		Moon	
Lagna Ketu			
Venus			Rahu Jupiter Mars
Sun Mercury			Sat.

Exalted *Pakshbali* Moon is in Kendra to Jupiter, lord of 2nd and 11th houses, and located in friendly sign in 7th house. It forms *Gajakesari Yoga* and destroys *Kemadruma Yoga*. There is also strong *Budha-Aditya Yoga* in 11th house. Location of Sun in 11th house during day birth adds strength to the horoscope. The lords of 7th and 11th houses, Sun and Jupiter respectively, exchange signs. Strong Moon, Mars (lord of 10th house) aspect 10th house. Rahu, in 7th *Kendra* with strong benefic Jupiter and 10th lord Mars, becomes favourable. The native became Municipal Councillor in Mumbai in November, 2006 elections, during Rahu *Dasa*-Mercury *Bhukti* at the age of 27 years.

(2) When in a horoscope the 10th lord is placed in an angle (*Kendra*), 9th, 2nd or 5th houses from Moon, then the native becomes rich like a king. The above horoscope also has this *Yoga*.

(3) *Chandradhi Yoga*

When benefics occupy 6th, 7th and 8th houses from the Moon, *Chandradhi Yoga* is formed. (From *Lagna* it is called *Lagnadhi Yoga*.) When the *Yoga* forming planets are not combust or aspected by, or conjoined with, malefics and Moon is not weak (*Pakshabalheen*), the *Yoga* produces best result. The native born in this *Yoga* is wealthy, prosperous and enjoys high status, is famous and highly esteemed. He has a long life. A blemish free *Chandradhi Yoga* is rare.

Mr. Bill Gates, DOB: 28.10.1955, 20.58 hrs., Seattle (USA).

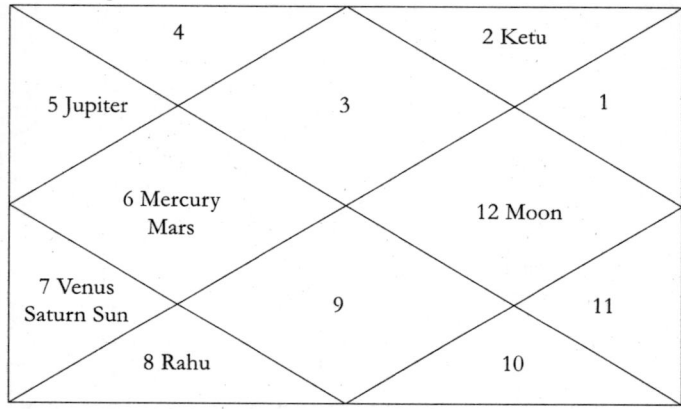

The 2nd house lord Moon is in 10th house. From Moon, Jupiter is in 6th house in friendly sign; exalted Mercury is in 7th house with Mars; and own sign Venus, with exalted Saturn and *Neechabhanga* Sun in 8th house. These form quite strong *Chandradhi Yoga*. Planets in *Kendra* to Moon nullify *Kemadruma Yoga*. The native is one of the richest Computer Magnate of the world.

(4) Shubha Yoga

When Jupiter and the Moon are in 2nd house, the 2nd lord in 11th house, and *Lagna* lord be in a benefic house, *Shubha Yoga* is formed. It makes the native very wealthy.

(5) Chandra Mangal Yoga

Mars in an angle (*Kendra*) with reference to the Moon forms this *Yoga*. It makes the native wealthy. The horoscope of Bill Gates displayed above has this *Yoga*. The Moon lord of 2nd house, and Mars lord of 11th house are posited in 10th and 4th houses respectively, i.e., in *Kendra* to each other. (*Note*: If these planets are weak or lord of evil house or located in malefic house, the native will have debased character and make money through dishonest means).

(6) Sakat Yoga

When Jupiter is located in the 6th or 8th place from the Moon, inauspicious *Sakat Yoga* is formed. An individual born with this *Yoga* is unfortunate, suffers mental agony, loses family wealth and becomes poor. *Sakat Yoga* becomes ineffective when Jupiter or Moon is in *Kendra* from *Lagna*.

IMPORTANCE OF SUN

The Sun is *Karka* (significator) for *Atma* (soul), father, courage, power, authority, status, mental sharpness and success in life. It gets *Digbala* (directional strength) in 10th house and confers best result. Strong Sun in the horoscope gives high status, name and fame to the native.

According to Astrological classics, when during a day birth Sun is posited in 11th house, it removes many deficiencies of the horoscope. Conversely, when the Sun is located in deep debilitation ($10°$ in Libra), other good *Yogas* in the horoscope become infructuous.

Sun Yogas

When benefics, other than Moon, Rahu and Ketu, occupy the 2nd or 12th house, or both side of the Sun, the *Yogas* formed respectively are called *Shubhavesi*, *Shubhavasi* and *Shubhyochari Yogas*. When these places are occupied by malefic planets, the *Yogas* formed are called *Ashubhavesi*, *Ashubhavasi* and *Ashubhayochari Yoga* respectively.

One born with *Shubhavesi Yoga* is handsome, happy, brave, victorious and successful.

One born with *Shubhavasi Yoga* becomes famous, popular, prosperous, liberal and favourite of the Government.

One born in *Shubhayochari Yoga* is handsome, prosperous, famous, and has impressive speech.

An individual born in *Ashubhavesi Yoga* vilifies others, and associates with low and wicked people.

An individual born in *Ashubhavasi Yoga* is deceitful, abusive, friend of wicked and does bad deeds.

An individual born in *Ashubhayochari Yoga* is mentally afflicted, infamous, devoid of learning, wealth and luck.

Late Sunil Dutt, Film Actor and Central Minister,

DOB: 6.6.1931, 11.30. A.M., Jhelum (Pakistan).

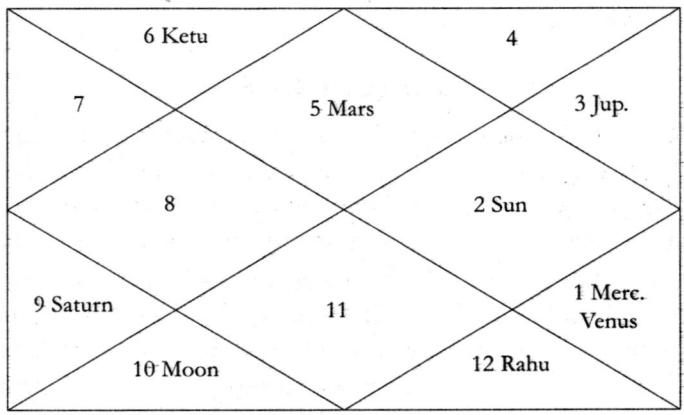

Important Planetary Yogas

Rahu	Merc. Venus	Sun	Jup.
Moon			Lagna Mars
Saturn			Ketu

Yoga karka Mars is posited in *Lagna*. *Lagna* lord Sun is *Uttarayan* (in the Northern course) and posited in 10th house where it gets *Digbala*.

In 12th to Sun, is 2nd and 11th lord Mercury with 10th lord Venus. In 2nd to Sun, is posited 5th lord Jupiter. These planets form *Shubhavesi, Shubhavasi* and *Shubhayochari Yogas*. The 10th house and *Lagna* lord Sun are also in *Shubhakartari Yoga*, making these strong.

After coming from Pakistan he took up small jobs, became Radio announcer, and later on entered films where he made his mark as an actor and a director. He was elected Member of Parliament five times, and at the time of his death was the Sports and Youth Minister at the Centre. He made steady progress in life and achieved great success, wealth and fame by virtue of favourable Sun *Yogas*.

Budha – *Aditya Yoga*

This *Yoga* is formed by the conjunction of the Sun and *Budha* (Mercury) in a house. As Mercury is never more than 28° away from the Sun, this *Yoga* is frequently found in the horoscopes. Though Mercury does not get combust in proximity to the Sun, experience shows that it gives good result when away from the Sun. This *Yoga* gives best result when it occurs in Aries, Gemini, Leo, Virgo and Sagittarius *Lagna* in a benefic house.

A strong *Budha – Aditya Yoga* makes the native successful as Counsellor, Lecturer, writer, scientist, lawyer, astrologer or accountant. When *Budha-Aditya Yoga* is formed in Gemini or Virgo sign in a *Kendra*, Mercury additionally forms *Bhadra Mahapurusha Yoga* which confers excellent success, wealth and fame.

Female, DOB: 5.7.1950, 05.00 A.M., Rajgarh (M.P.).

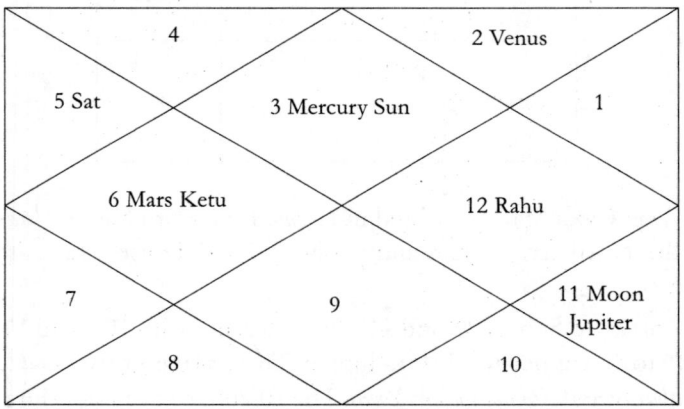

The horoscope has *Budha-Aditya* and *Bhadra Mahapurusha Yoga* in Gemini *Lagna*. There is *Gajkesari Yoga* in 9th house formed by 2nd lord Moon and 7th and 10th lord Jupiter. The *Yoga* is aspected by 9th lord Saturn. Jupiter is *Vargottam* and aspects *Lagna* and 5th house. There is exchange of aspect between 9th lord Saturn and 10th lord Jupiter forming *Dharma Karmadhipati Yoga*. *Vargottam* Venus in own sign in 12th house is auspicious for prosperity. Saturn and Moon are exalted in *Navamsa*. In *Dasmasa* Chart, Mercury is exalted in Virgo *Lagna*, and Venus and Jupiter are in 10th house aspected by Sun.

She started with giving tuitions at home in Saturn *Dasa*-Jupiter *Bhukti*. With the start of Mercury *Dasa* she opened a Primary School which has developed into Hr. Secondary School. Construction of building for college is in progress.

Combined Effect of Strong *Lagna*, Sun and Moon

According to *Saravali*, if *Lagna* lord and Moon sign lord are strong and conjoined in *Kendra*, while Moon occupies watery sign in a *Trine* (5,9), the native becomes a king (enjoys very high status).

When the *Lagna* lord, the Sun and Moon occupy a *Kendra* or *Trikona*, in exaltation, own or friendly sign, the resultant *Yoga* is *Srikanta*. Such native is very religious, mentally and spiritually strong, and great worshipper of Lord Shiva.

According to *Phalitmartand*, "When *Lagna* is *vargottam*, Moon is *Vargottam*, and *Atmakarka* (planet with highest degree) is strong; there is a strong planet is *Kenara* and a benefic planet in 2nd house to Sun, it is a lucky birth."

Shri Chandrasekhar, former P.M.,
DOB: 17.4.1927, 5.32 AM, Ballia (U.P.).

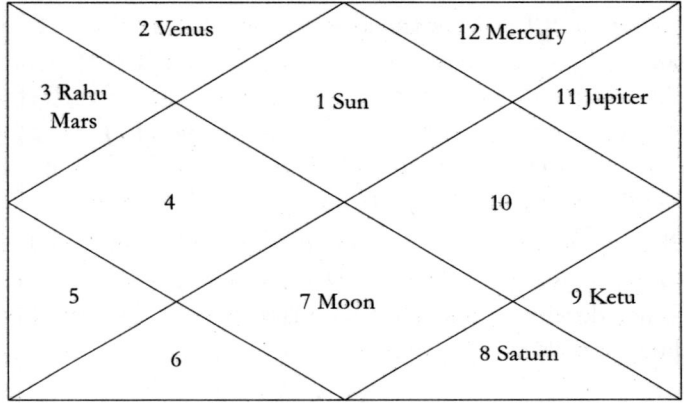

Lagna is in *Shubha kartari Yoga* and *Vargottam*. 5th lord Sun in *Uttarayan* is exalted in *Lagna*. *Swakshetri* (own sign) Venus in 2nd and Mercury in 12th to Sun form *Shubhayochari Yoga*. Mars is in 3rd house aspected by 9th lord Jupiter. Moon is *Pakshabali*, *Vargottam* and aspected by Jupiter. The *Lagna*, Moon and Sun are very strong. He rose from a student leader gradually and became Prime Minister of India.

Rajyogas

The inter-connection of planets in the following groups form *Rajyoga:*

(1) Planets in their exaltation, *Mooltrikona*, own sign, friend's sign and *Trikonas* (1, 5, 9).
(2) Planets in *Kendras* (1, 4, 7, 10) and *Vargottam*.
(3) Planets that own a *Trikona* and a *Kendra* (*Yoga karka*).
(4) Planets aspected by benefics, and those between benefics.

Provided the *Yoga* forming planets should not own 8th or 11th house.

The *Rajyogas* formed by *Kendra* and *Trikona* lords produce the best result as under:

(1) The lords of *Lagna* and 4th house confer happiness, property and vehicles.
(2) The lords of *Lagna* and 5th house make one intelligent, learned and wealthy.
(3) The lords of *Lagna* and 7th house make the native virtuous and the person gets a capable spouse.
(4) The lords of *Lagna* and 9th house make one lucky, religious, wealthy and happy.
(5) The lords of *Lagna* and 10th house make one successful, of high status, and famous.
(6) The lords of 5th and 4th houses make one happy with own ability.
(7) The lords of 5th and 7th houses give an intelligent spouse and he leads a happy married life, with success in business.
(8) The lords of 5th and 9th houses make one capable, lucky, learned, wealthy and happy.
(9) The lords of 5th and 10th houses make one successful in administrative work, and he holds a high status and is wealthy.

(10) The lords of 9th and 4th houses make one lucky and happy in every way.

(11) The lords of 9th and 7th houses give considerate spouse, and the native leads a happy life after his marriage.

(12) The lords of 9th and 10th houses make one lucky, happy, wealthy, with high status. This *Yoga* is considered the best for worldly success, provided the 9th lord is not the lord of 8th, and the 10th lord does not own 11th house as well.

Thus the *Yogas* formed by *Kendra* and *Trikona* lords confer wealth, happiness and prosperity in varying degree as elucidated above.

Dhana Yogas

When two or more of the lords of *Lagna*, 2nd, 5th, 9th and 11th houses become mutually related by conjunction, aspect or exchange of signs, and if these are strong, the native will be very wealthy.

Shri R.P. Goenka, Industrialist,

DOB: 1.3.1930, 8.45 A.M., Kolkata.

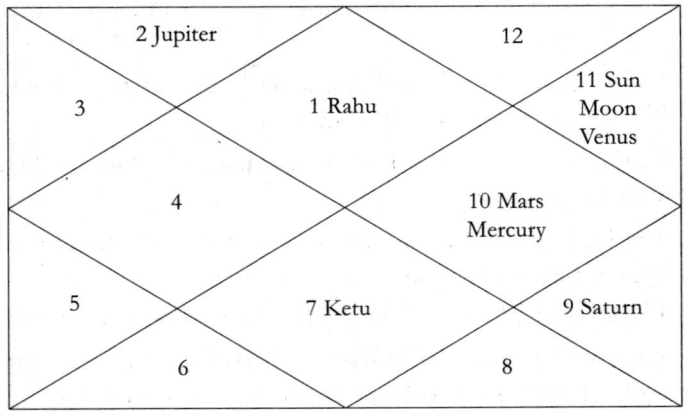

Important Planetary Yogas

	Lagna Rahu	Jup.	
Sun Moon Venus			
Mars Merc.			
Sat.		Ketu	

Lagna lord Mars is exalted in 10th house forming *Ruchuk* and *Kuldeepak Yogas*. Mars is conjoined with Mercury (lord of two *Upachaya* houses) which gives the native capability to work intelligently with full confidence to achieve his goal. Rahu in *Lagna* in Aries gives shrewd and secretive personality. The 10th and 11th lord Saturn is posited in 9th house, and 9th lord Jupiter by its aspect on 10th house crowns native's efforts with success. Jupiter in 2nd house and Moon in 11th house form benefic *Gajkesari Yoga*. Lord of 2nd in 11th, lord of 11th in 9th, and 9th lord in 2nd house form strong *Dhana Yoga*. Lords of 2nd, 4th, 5th and 7th houses are posited in 11th house of gains, and are aspected by the 10th and 11th lord Saturn posited in 9th house, thereby increasing his prosperity. His Venus *Dasa* started in March, 1985 and gave him much prosperity. However, being lord of 2nd and 7th (*Marka*) houses, the native also suffered serious health problems. From March, 2005 has started the 5th lord Sun *Dasa* which is posited in 11th and will add to his name, fame and prosperity.

But if the lord of any of the evil house (6, 8, 12) be related to *Dhana Yoga*, then the wealth is lost, the native incurs debt and faces troubles through enemies, and by his wrong action. Such result will appear in the major period of lords of 2nd, 5th, 9th or 11th houses forming *Dhana Yoga*.

Wealth Giving Special *Yogas*

1. **Vasuman Yoga:** When auspicious planets are posited in *Upachaya* (3, 6, 10 and 11) houses either from *Lagna* or Moon, these form *Vasuman Yoga*. Such an individual becomes very rich with little effort.

2. **Rajpad Yoga:** When *Lagna* or Moon is *Vargottama* and aspected by benefic planets, this *Yoga* is formed. It makes the person wealthy like a King.

3. **Amla Yoga:** When there are auspicious planets in 10th house from *Lagna* or the Moon, this *Yoga* is formed. Such a native is learned, rich, prosperous and famous.

4. **Shubha Yoga:** When Jupiter and Moon are in 2nd house, the 2nd lord is in 11th house, and *Lagna* lord be in a benefic house, this *Yoga* is formed. It makes the person very rich.

5. **Lakshmi Yoga:** When the lord of 9th house and Venus are posited in their own or exaltation sign identical with a *Kendra* or *Trikona*, then this *Yoga* is formed. Such *Yoga* gives health, wealth, blessings of Goddess Lakshmi, and the individual enjoys best luxuries and vehicles in life.

6. **Pushkal Yoga:** When the lord of Moon sign is in association with *Lagna* lord in an angle or in the house of a very friendly planet, and if an auspicious strong planet aspects the *Lagna*, then this *Yoga* is formed. The native born with this *Yoga* is soft spoken, gentle, wealthy and famous.

7. **Kuber Tulya Yoga:** If Jupiter and Venus are exalted and posited in *Kendra* or *Trikona*, then the native of royal birth becomes a King, and one born in any other family becomes very wealthy.

8. **Guru Mangal Yoga:** If Jupiter is in 2nd house in own sign along with Mars, this *Yoga* is formed. Such a native becomes very rich in life. (This is possible in Scorpio and Aquarius *Lagna*. But as Mars is also 6th lord in Scorpio *Lagna*, and 3rd lord in Aquarius *Lagna* there may be some loss as well).

Other famous *Yogas*

1. **Mala Yoga:** If all the natural benefics are located in *Kendras*, *Mala Yoga* is formed. Such an individual is learned, wealthy and happy.
2. **Sarpa Yoga:** If all the natural malefics are in *Kendras*, *Sarpa Yoga* is formed. Such a native suffers from poverty and troubles, gives trouble to others, and is short lived.
3. **Mangla Yoga:** If all the planets (Sun to Saturn) be in *Kendras*, *Mangla Yoga* is formed. Such native is intelligent, long lived and does good deeds.
4. **Varaha Yoga:** If all the planets are located in the 1st, 4th and 5th houses, *Varaha Yoga* is formed. Such native is a leader, wealthy and happy.
5. **Sankha Yoga:** If all the planets occupy the 1st, 4th, 9th and 11th houses, *Sankha Yoga* is formed. Such a person is virtuous and brave.
6. **Chakra Yoga:** If all the planets occupy six odd signs (Aries, Gemini, Leo, etc.) *Chakra Yoga* is formed. Such a person has good qualities and owns landed property.
7. **Samudra Yoga:** If all the planets are posited from 2nd house in six *Rasis*, intervened by a planetless *Rasi* (i.e., planets are in 2nd, 4th, 6th, 8th, 10th and 12th houses, and intervening houses have no planets) this *Yoga* is formed. Such a person is a miser but wealthy.
8. **Indira Yoga:** When all the planets be posited from 2nd house with two house planetless in between, *Indira Yoga* is formed. Such a person is famous, wealthy and enjoys high status.
9. **Kedar Yoga:** When the 7 planets are in any four *Rasis*, *Kedar Yoga* is formed. Such a person is dutiful, earns by agriculture, helps his relatives and is honoured.
10. **Parvat Yoga:** When all the *Kendras* and 9th house are occupied by planets and 8th and 12th houses are vacant, this *Yoga* is formed. Such an individual is virtuous, and his fame lasts even after his death.

11. **Dhwaja Yoga:** When all the planets are in 10th house and *Lagna*, *Dhwaja Yoga* is formed. Such a native is wise, courageous, wealthy and famous.
12. **Shatpada Yoga:** When all the planets occupy the first six signs *Shatpada Yoga* is formed. Such a person is a leader, learned and wealthy.
13. **Shubha Mala Yoga:** When all the benefics occupy the 5th, 6th and 7th houses this *Yoga* is formed. Such native is a capable leader, administrator, helpful to co-workers and enjoys life with wife and sons.
14. **Ashubha Mala Yoga:** When the benefics occupy the 6th, 8th and. 12th houses the *Yoga* formed is *Ashubhmala*. Such a person is timid, unhappy, ungrateful, quarrelsome and falls to evil ways.

Yoga Bhanga
(Destruction of Benefic *Yogas*)

The *Yogas* formed by the following planets do not produce benefic result:

(1) Debilitated Planets.

(2) Planets in inimical signs.

(3) Planet with, aspected by, or in between malefics.

(4) Planets in *Bhava Sandhi*.

(5) Planets eclipsed by the Sun or Rahu.

(6) Planets having less than 5 *Rupas* in *Shadabala*.

(7) Planets defeated in mutual war.

(8) Lords of 6th, 8th or 12th houses with lords of *Kendra* and *Trikona*.

(9) If all the malefics occupy *Kendras,* identical with their debilitation or inimical sign, while benefics are located in 6th, 8th or 12th houses.

The benefic *Yogas* in the horoscope also become ineffective:

(i) When the Sun or the Moon is located in extreme debilitation degree, and

(ii) When the *Lagna* and the Moon sign are not aspected by any benefic planet.

OTHER NOTABLE *YOGAS*

(1) *Panch Mahapurusha Yogas*

When in the horoscope Mars, Mercury, Jupiter, Venus and Saturn (each of them) occupy an angle (*Kendra*) identical with its own or exaltation sign, these form five powerful *Yogas*. These *Yogas* are respectively called *Ruchuk, Bhadra, Hamsa, Malavya* and *Sasa Yoga*. As these *Yogas* give lasting wealth, fame, prosperity and long life to the person having such *Yoga* in his horoscope, these are called *Panch Mahapurusha Yogas*. When these *Yogas* are also formed from Moon's position, the benefic result increases manifold. However, if the *Yoga* forming planets are afflicted or weak in *Navamsa*, or if the Sun is conjoined with the Moon in the horoscope, only ordinary results are experienced by the person.

A person born with *Ruchuk Yoga* (formed by Mars) has long face and strong body. He is brave, proud conquers his enemies, and acquires wealth through daring actions. He may be a brave and daring officer in Army or Police, who is famous for his meritorious deeds.

A person born with *Bhadra Yoga* (formed by Mercury) has quick grasp, is learned, talented, well versed in *Shastras*, honest, rich, quick in decision making, and has impressive speech.

A person born with *Hamsa Yoga* (formed by Jupiter) has good voice, is righteous, learned, rich, generous and admired by all.

A person born with *Malavya Yoga* (formed by Venus) is handsome with beautiful figure, good features, pleasing manners, wise, learned, wealthy, famous, has good conveyances, and enjoys life with his family.

A person born with *Sasa Yoga* (formed by Saturn) is tall, strong, learned, rich, famous, dealer in minerals, a leader or headman, with faithful servants.

As regards the result of these *Pancha Mahapurusha Yogas* the native born with one such *Yoga* will be fortunate, with two; like a king, with three; a king, with 4 such *Yogas;* King of Kings, and with five such *Yogas* world famous.

(1) Male, DOB: 20.9.1954, 3.55 P.M., Amritsar.

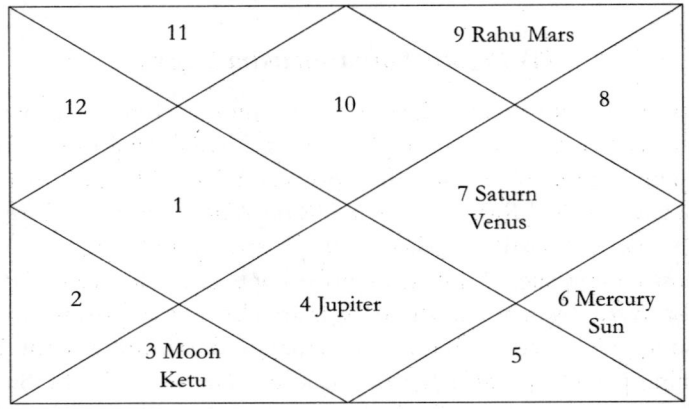

Jupiter, Saturn and Venus respectively form *Hamsa, Sasa* and *Malavya Yogas* from *Lagna*. Mercury forms *Bhadra Yoga* from Moon. Jupiter and Saturn have highest *Shadabala.* Jupiter is *Vargottama,* Venus is exalted, and Saturn is in own sign in *Navamsa* Chart. The 9th lord

Important Planetary Yogas

Mercury in *Lagna* Chart is exalted in 9th house, and forms *Buddha-Aditya Yoga*. The native had about 6 years' balance of Rahu *Dasa* at birth, which was followed by Jupiter, Saturn and Mercury *Dasas* forming *Panch Mahapurusha Yogas*.

The native is a reputed exporter of kitchen items, machine tools, and books with yearly turn over in crores.

(2) Male, DOB: 23.10.1954, 11.37.P.M., Bulandshahar (U.P.)

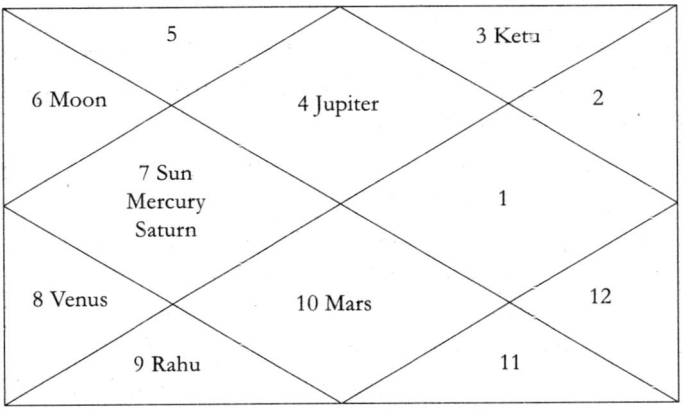

Jupiter, Saturn and Mars exalted in *Kendra* from *Lagna* form *Hamsa, Sasa* and *Ruchuk Panch Mahapurusha Yoga* respectively. There is also *Buddha-Aditya Yoga* in the 4th house with cancellation of debilitation of the Sun.

The native was born in a middle class family and completed his C.A. in record time with good division. At the start of Jupiter *Dasa* in 1992 he got an opening in a Dubai based MNC. He is Head of Accounts Division now drawing huge pay package.

(2) *Mahabhagya Yoga*

This is formed differently in the case of males and females as under:
(i) During day birth of males, if the *Lagna*, Sun and the Moon are located in odd signs.
(ii) During night birth of females, if the *Lagna*, the Sun and the Moon are located in even signs.

Such an individual enjoys everlasting fame, takes to virtuous ways, is kind hearted, respected by all and brings credit to his family. The individual is famous and remembered for a long time after death. For full benefic result the *Lagna*, Sun and Moon should be strong.

This *Yoga* was present in the horoscope of Shri Morarji Desai and Smt. Indira Gandhi, former Prime Ministers of India. The *Yoga* is present in the horoscope of Mrs. Shabana Azmi, Film Actress and Member of Rajya Sabha, which is discussed below.

Female, DOB: 18.9.1949, 7.15 P.M., Hyderabad.

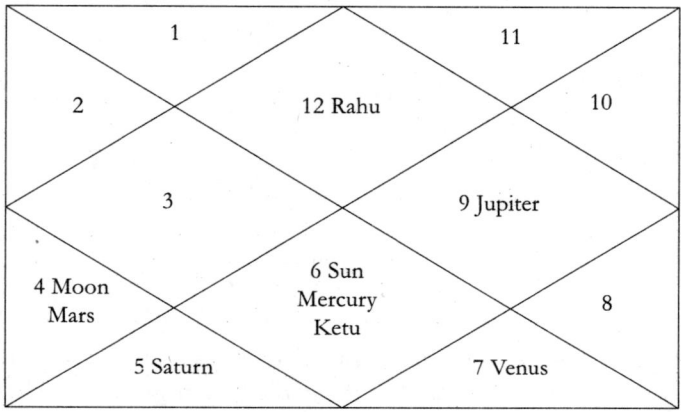

Lagna Rahu			
			Moon Mars
			Saturn
Jupiter		Venus	Sun Mercury Ketu

Lagna, Moon and Sun are in even *Rasi* for female birth during night and form *Mahabhagya Yoga*. *Lagna* falls in Pisces, and its lord Jupiter in 10th house in own sign, forms *Hamsa Yoga*. 5th lord Moon is in own sign Cancer with 9th lord Mars who gets *Neecha Bhanga*. Sun is in Virgo in 7th house with exalted Mercury and forms *Buddha-Aditya Yoga*. Moon and Mars form *Chandra-Mangal* benefic *Yoga* in 5th house.

She is a famous film actress, a Member of Rajya Sabha, and associated with many social organizations. She has been conferred Honorary Doctorate Degree by many foreign Universities.

(3) *Parivartana Yoga*

As the name suggests, this *Yoga* denotes mutual exchange between the lords of two houses. For example, in Sagittarius *Lagna* Mars in Pisces (Jupiter's sign) and Jupiter in Aries (Mars' sign) constitute *Parivartana Yoga*.

The exchange of houses by *Kendra* and *Trikona* lords forms excellent *Rajyoga* which helps the native rise in life during the *dasabhukti* of planets forming the *Yoga*, provided the planets are not weak or afflicted. As the 9th house is the best *Trikona* and 10th house is the best *Kendra*, exchange of their lords gives best *Rajyoga* and confers status, wealth, name and fame. The exchange between other *Trikona* and *Kendra* lords (5/4, 5/10, etc.) rank next in result. *Parivartana Yogas* formed by lords of benefic houses are invariably found in the horoscope of successful persons.

The result of *Parivartana Yoga* in brief is as follows:

(i) Exchange by strong and unafflicted lords of two benefic houses produces very good result. It is also called '*Mahayoga*.'

(ii) Exchange of a benefic house lord with that of 6th, 8th or 12th houses lord causes problems, financial stringency and loss of wealth. It is called '*Dainya Yoga*'.

(iii) However, exchange by lords of malefic (6, 8, 12) houses produces good result. It is called *Vipreet Rajyoga*. Further affliction of these planets increases good result.

(1) Gurudev Rabindra Nath Tagore,
    DOB: 7.5.1861, 2.51 A.M., Calcutta.

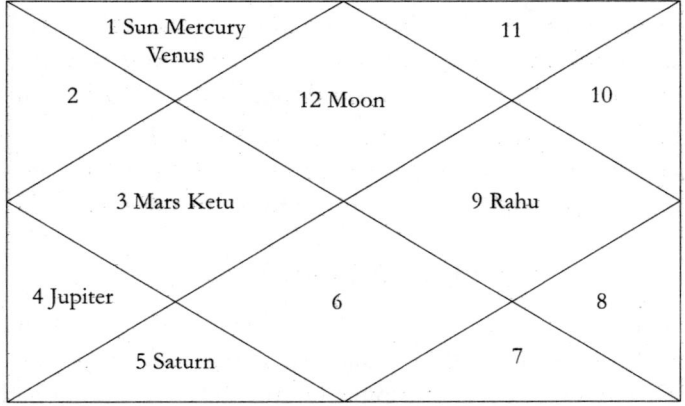

Lagna Moon	Sun Mercury Venus		Mars Ketu
			Jupiter
			Sat.
Rahu			

The horoscope has the following *Parivartana Yogas:*

(i) Between exalted *Lagna* lord Jupiter in 5th, and 5th lord Moon in *Lagna* – very good.

(ii) Between Mars, lord of 2nd and 9th, and Mercury lord of 4th and 7th houses – very good.

He was a world famous poet, painter and philosopher, and was awarded prestigious Nobel Prize for Literature in 1913 (Moon-Mercury). He founded Vishwabharti University in 1921 (Mars-Venus). The horoscope has some other good *Yogas*, namely, *Saraswati, Chamar, Chhatra* and *Vimal Yogas*, which helped him rise in life and become world famous.

(2) Smt. Indira Gandhi, former P.M.,
DOB: 19.11.1917, 23.11 hrs., Allahabad.

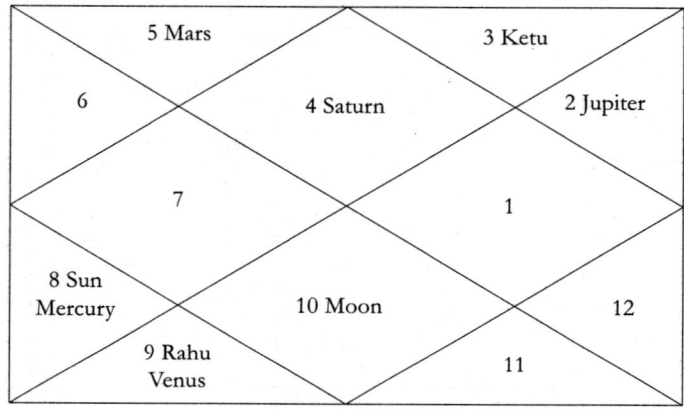

There are three *Parivartana Yogas* in the horoscope:

(i) Between *Yoga karka* Mars, lord of 5th and 10th, with the Sun, lord of 2nd house. – very good.

(ii) Between Jupiter lord of 9th and 6th, and Venus, lord of 4th and 11th very good.

(iii) Between Saturn, lord of 7th and 8th, and Moon, lord of *Lagna*. – Mixed.

She became Member of Parliament in 1964 (Jupiter - Venus), and joined as I & B Minister in Shri Lal Bahadur's Cabinet. After his death, she became Prime Minister in 1966 (Jupiter - Sun) till she lost election after imposition of emergency in 1977 (Saturn - Ketu). She regained office in 1980 (Saturn - Venus) and occupied it till her assassination on 31.10.1984 (Saturn - Rahu) by her Sikh bodyguards. Saturn is *Maraka,* Rahu is debilitated in 6th house, and these are placed in 6/8 position.

There is no exalted planet in the horoscope or *Panch Mahapurusha Yoga,* yet Mrs. Gandhi attained phenomenal success and international stature due to the *Parivartana Yogas* in her horoscope.

(4) Vipreet Rajyoga

The lords of evil (6th, 8th and 12th) houses by their nature and effect cause distress and difficulties to the individual concerned. When the lords of these houses are strong and occupy *Kenara* or *Trikona* house, and the lords of *Lagna*, 10th, 4th and 9th houses, are weak or elipsed and posited in the 6th 8th or 12th houses it is a *Duryoga (Phaladeepika,* VI. 70).

But when the lords of these *Trika* (evil) houses become mutually connected through exchange of houses, mutual aspect or conjuction in these very houses, and are further aspected by malefics, the *yoga* makes the native prosperous, powerful, long lived and famous like a king. Because of the nature of *Yoga* forming planets producing excellent result, it is called *Virpreet Rajyoga.* While malefic aspect increases benefic result, any benefic aspect is counter – productive.

The specific result of different *Vipreet Rajyogas* formed by the lords of 6th, 8th and 12th houses are as under:

(1) When the lord of 6th house occupies an evil (6th, 8th, 12th) house, and is associated with, or aspected by, malefics the *Vipreet Rajyoga* is called *Harsh Yoga.* A person born with such *Yoga* is lucky, healthy, happy, wins over enemies, and refrains from sinful acts. The person is blessed with wealth, splendour, fame, friends and sons (*Phaladeepika,* VI.63).

(2) When the lord of 8th house is posited in evil (6th, 8th, 12th) house and is associated with, or aspected by malefics the *Vipreet Rajyoga*

formed is called *Saral Yoga*. A person born in this *Yoga* is determined, fearless, learned, wealthy, prosperous and has long life. He is successful in all his enterprises, overcomes enemies and is widely respected. (*ibid*, VI.65).

(3) When the lord of 12th house occupies an evil (6, 8, 12) house and is associated with, or aspected by, malefics the *Vipreet Rajyoga* formed is called *Vimal Yoga*. Such an individual spends much less than what he earns, pursues a respectable profession, is good to everybody, independent, happy and well known for his merits. (*ibid*, VI.69).

(1) Female, DOB: 27.12.1937, 11 P.M., Delhi.

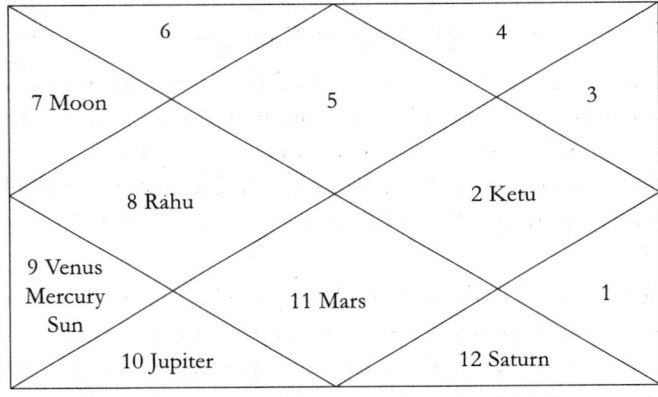

Important Planetary Yogas 135

In this horoscope, the lord of 6th house Saturn, and lord of 8th house Jupiter exchange houses. Jupiter is debilitated and aspected by Ketu, and Saturn is aspected by Rahu. As a result of the *Vipreet Rajyoga* formed by the lords of 6th and 8th houses, the lady is very rich, prosperous and long lived.

She had Rahu *Dasa* at birth upto 27. 10. 1940, followed by Jupiter *Dasa* upto 1956, and then Saturn *Dasa* upto 1975, both forming *Vipreet Rajyoga*. She then had favourable Mercury *dasa* (exalted in *Navamsa*) upto 1992, followed by Venus *Dasa* upto 2012, (*Kendra* lord in *Trikona*). However, Venus, in *Navamsa* is 7th and 12th lord posited in 7th (*maraka*) house, and *Sade-sati* has started on 10th September, 2009.

(5) *Neecha Bhanga Rajyoga*

According to *Phaladeepika*:

नीचे ग्रहेऽध: पतनं स्ववृत्तेदैन्यं दुराचारमृण‍प्तिमाहु:।
नीचाश्रयं कीकटदेशवासं भृत्यत्वमध्वानमनर्थकार्यम् ॥

meaning, "Should a planet be in debilitation in a birth chart, that native will suffer during its *Dasa* period degradation from his position, humiliation, do sinful acts, undergo debts, look for help from low people, live in unhealthy places and do menial work, travel long distances and perform evil deeds."

Thus in the normal course a debilitated planet in the horoscope spoils the affairs of the house owned and occupied by it, and causes many problems during its *Dasa-Bhukti*. However, on fulfillment of certain conditions, the debilitated planet loses its debilitation, gets revitalized with the help of other planets, and confers benefic result, no less than a *Rajyoga*. Because of the manner of formation of this Yoga and its benefic result, it is called *Neecha Bhanga Rajyoga* (NBRY). The conditions for cancellation of debilitation, applicable to all *Bhava* lords mentioned in astrological treatises are as under:-

(1) The debilitated planet is in *Kendra* from *Lagna* or the Moon.
(2) The debilitated planet is aspected by its dispositor (the lord of the sign where debilitated).

(3) The dispositor of the debilitated planet is in *Kendra* from *Lagna* or the Moon.

(4) The planet that is exalted in the sign where the debilitated planet is located, is in *Kendra* to the *Lagna* or the Moon.

(5) The lord of the sign in which the debilitated planet gets exalted, is in *Kendra* to the *Lagna* or the Moon.

(6) The lord of the debilitation sign and the lord of the exaltation sign of the planet in question are mutually in *Kendra* position.

Though, the Astrological classics do not elaborate further, it is logical to presume that the effect of cancellation obtained will correspond to the strength of the planet that brings about the cancellation of debilitation. The result of NBRY may not be identical in all cases, but it does remove the effect of debilitation to a great extent, and improves the native's life, status and wealth as is evident from the following horoscopes.

(1) Count Louis Hamon (Cheiro),
   DOB: 1.11.1866, 10.05 A.M., London.

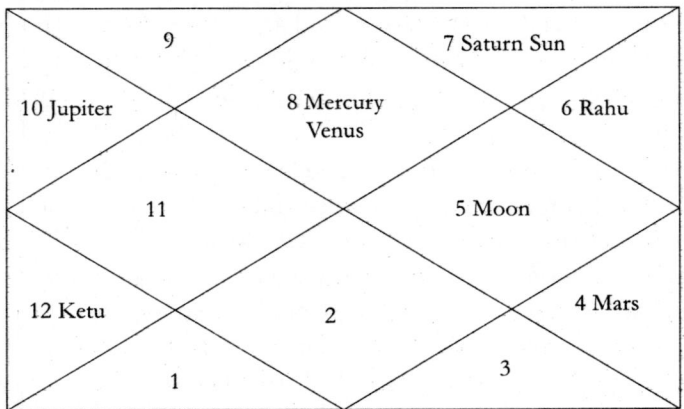

Important Planetary Yogas

Ketu			
			Mars
Jupiter			Moon
	Lagna Mercury Venus	Saturn Sun	Rahu

This is the horoscope of world famous astrologer, palmist and numerologist. Three planets – *Lagna* lord Mars, 2nd and 5th lord Jupiter, and 10th lord Sun are debilitated in the horoscope.

Mars' debilitation gets cancelled as its dispositor Moon is in *Kendra* from *Lagna*. Jupiter attains *Neecha Bhanga* as Moon, the lord of the sign where Jupiter gets exalted, is in *Kendra* from *Lagna*. The Sun also attains *Neecha Bhanga* as its dispositor Venus is in *Kendra* from *Lagna* and the Moon. The Sun is also with exalted Saturn. Thus the debilitation of these three planets (Mars, Jupiter and Sun) gets cancelled. These planets located in *Kendra* from each other form *Karak Yoga* and cooperate to lift the native in life.

During Sun, Moon and Mars *Dasas*, associated with 9th, 10th and 12th houses, Cheiro came to India (Varanasi) to learn Astrology, Numerology and Palmistry. After his return to U.K. he published his famous book "*The World Predictions*" in 1925 in Rahu *Dasa* – Venus *Bhukti*. Rahu is in 11th house aspected by Jupiter, lord of 2nd and 5th house, located in 3rd house. Venus is in *Lagna* with 11th lord Mercury. Many of the predictions made in the book came true and he became world famous.

(2) Film Actor Devanand,
    DOB: 26.9.1923, 9.30 A.M., Gurdaspur (Punjab).

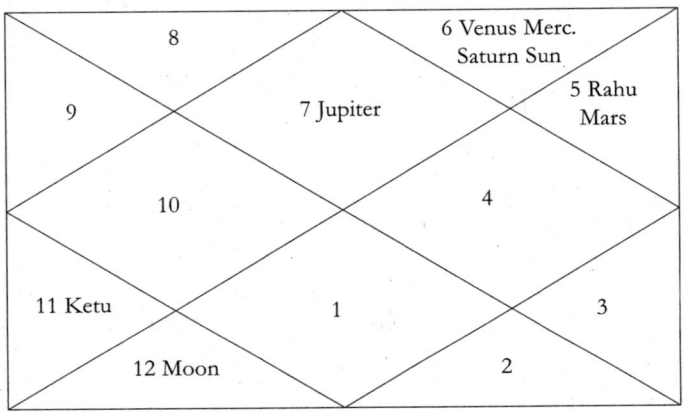

The active octogenarian film actor/producer got his autobiography titled '*Romancing with Life*' released by Prime Minster Dr. Manmohan Singh in the presence of Smt. Sonia Gandhi at Delhi on his 85th birthday.

Lagna is artistic sign Libra with benefic Jupiter posited there. However, *Lagna* lord Venus is debilitated in 12th house conjoined with exalted Mercury in *Kendra* to Moon which cancels its debilitation. Venus is conjoined with *Yoga karka* Saturn and Sun. These are aspected by full Moon from 6th house, which further invigorates the planets in 12th house. Venus in 12th house is reputed to give prosperity, except in Saturn's sign in *Lagna* or *Navamsa* Charts. The location of Venus and Mercury in 7th, and Jupiter in 8th, from Moon form prosperous *Chandradhi Yoga*. Venus, as 8th lord in 12th, also forms *Saral Vipreet Rajoyga*.

He came to Mumbai at the age of 19 years and after some struggle got a break in films in 1945 during Venus *Dasa*-Sun *Bhukti*. His first film *Hum Ek Hain* on Hindu-Muslim unity was released during Venus-Moon, just after independence. After many hit films, he started producing his own films as romantic hero and became fashion idol for youth. His success decreased during Rahu *Dasa* which started in 1984. Rahu is with Mars in 11th house in inimical sign and is not aspected by any benefic planet. During Jupiter *Dasa* (lord of 3rd and 6th houses) in *Lagna*, which started in 2002 he produced some unsuccessful films. He has been awarded prestigeous *Dada Sahab Phalke Award* for life time achievements in films.

Hence, one should not get disturbed by seeing debilitated planets in horoscope, but deeply examine it and *Dasa-Bhukti* sequence before arriving at any conclusion.

(6) *Malika Yoga*

All planets continuously occupying four, five, six or seven houses are described as *Malika* (garland) *Yoga*. It confers progressively greater success upon the native as the planets are posited continuously in more number of houses. But the effect of the placement starting from houses 8th or 12th is not desirable. These are tabulated below for easy comprehension. Rahu and Ketu are not taken into consideration.

Yoga	Starting From	Result
Malika	*Lagna*	*Rajyoga*
Dhana Malika	House 2	Wealthy or scholar
Vikram Malika	House 3	Successful
Bandhu Malika	House 4	Praiseworthy
Mantri Malika	House 5	*Rajyoga*
Indra Malika	House 6	*Rajyoga*
Kaama Malika	House 7	Blissful
Nidhana Malika	House 8	Loser or short lived
Shubha Malika	House 9	Fortunate
Keerti Malika	House 10	Renowned
Vijaya Malika	House 11	Highly gainful
Patana Malika	House 12	Debacles

Thus *Malika Yoga* starting from houses 8th or 12th is not desirable.

(1) Bill Clinton, President of USA,
DOB: 19.8.1946, 5.00 A.M., Arkansas (USA).

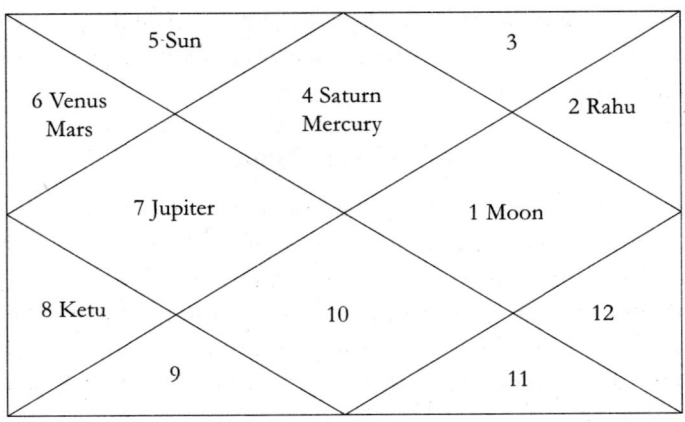

Important Planetary Yogas

	Moon	Rahu	
			Lagna Saturn Merc
			Sun
	Ketu	Jupiter	Venus Mars

Six Planets are located from *Lagna* to 4th house forming *Malika Yoga*. There are also *Gajakesari, Ubhayochari* and *Chandradhi Yoga* in the horoscope.

(2) Shri Rattan Tata, Industrialist,
    DOB: 28.12.1937, 6.30 A.M., Mumbai.

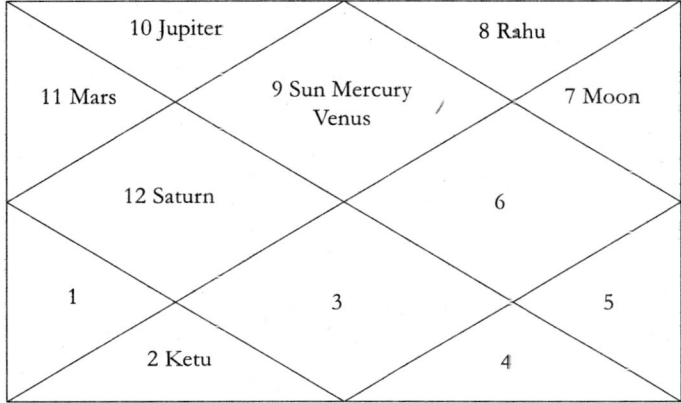

Saturn		Ketu	
Mars			
Jupiter			
Lagna Sun Mercury Venus	Rahu	Moon	

Six planets are posited from *Lagna* to 4th house forming *Malika Yoga*. There is conjunction of 9th, 10th and 11th lords in *Lagna*, and exchange of 2nd and 4th lords. There is also *Vesi Yoga* and *Gajakesari Yoga*.

(7) *Daridra Yoga* (Poverty)

When the lords of *Lagna*, 2nd (wealth) and 11th (gains) houses are associated with, or aspected by malefics or these have connection with *Trika* (6th, 8th, 12th) houses, or their lords, then it causes *Daridra Yoga*. The native faces financial stringency, loss of wealth, incurs debt and faces many problems in life.

If the 2nd house contains a malefic planet, and the lord of 2nd house is associated with, or aspected by, malefic planets the native hurts others by his speech and earns his livelihood with much difficulty.

When there are many malefics in 2nd house, the 2nd house lord is weak and aspected by malefics, and the lord of *Lagna* is placed in 6th, 8th or 12th houses with malefics, the native has no comforts in life.

If the lord of 2nd house is debilitated or eclipsed by the Sun, and if there are malefic planets in the 2nd and 8th houses, the native remains in debt.

Important Planetary Yogas

If the lord of 12th house is in 2nd house, and the lord of 11th house is in 12th, the lord of 2nd house is in 6th, 8th or 12th houses, or is in debilitation, the native loses wealth through punishment from Government.

If the 9th, 10th and 11th house lords are in their signs of debilitation and are afflicted by malefics, then even the individual born in royal family becomes poor.

If three or more planets are in debilitation or combust in a horoscope the native remains restless, troubled by enemies and devoid of wealth.

Male, DOB: 11.8.1963, 5.05 P.M., Delhi.

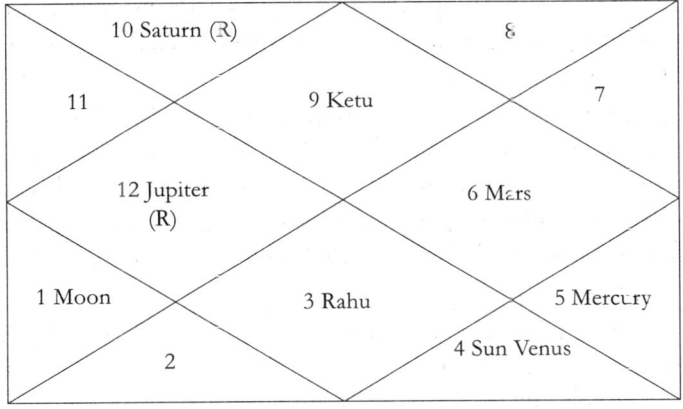

The *Lagna* lord Jupiter and *Karka* for wealth is retrograde in own sign in 4th house and forms *Hans Panch Mahapurusha Yoga*. It is aspected by the 2nd lord Saturn and 5th lord Mars. The native was born in a rich family. As the 11th lord Venus is combust by 9th lord Sun in the 8th house, and aspected by Saturn, the native lost several lakhs in shares during Sun *dasa* – Venus *Bhukti*.

(8) Arishta Yoga

The word *'Arishta'* is a synonym of *'Kashta'* which means physical pain, including death. Death occurring upto 12th year is called *Balarishta;* from 12th to 20th year is called *Yogarishta;* from 20th to 32nd years is called *Alpayu;* from 32 to 64 years is called *Madhyamayu;* and beyond that is called *Poornayu*.

When the *Lagna* or Moon or both are badly afflicted without any benefic aspect, it indicates *Balarishta*. When Moon is weak (near Sun) or when it is located in 6th, 8th or 12th houses, conjoined with or aspected by malefics it causes *Balarishta*. If all the malefic planets are posited in *Lagna* or the 7th *(Maraka)* house, there is danger of death of the child and the mother.

If Moon is in between malefic planets in 4th, 7th or 8th houses, and malefics are also located in *Lagna*, 7th and 8th houses, the native dies with the mother.

If the Moon is in *Lagna* with Rahu and another malefic without any benefic aspect, the native dies along with his mother.

To counter *Balarishta,* astrological treatises recommend *Mahamrityunjaya Japa* and *homa* every year on birth *Tithi* till he crosses 12th year, and to take prompt medical help whenever the child falls sick.

Arishta Bhanga

When there is a strong and full Moon between benefics in *Lagna* or other benefic house, it destroys every kind of *Arishta*.

When Mercury or any benefic planet is posited in *Lagna*, and the Sun is in 11th house, then all *Arishtas* are destroyed.

When Jupiter is in own or exaltation sign in *Lagna*, it removes many *Arishtas* caused by other planets.

When benefic planets are in own or *Mooltrikona* or exaltation sign, then all types of *Arishtas* are destroyed.

Chapter XI

Timing of Events

The exercise of divining future comprises three main steps — (i) casting of horoscope for the correct time, date and place of birth of the person; (ii) Assessment of the potential of horoscope (strength of different houses and planets); and (iii) When that potential will materialize in the form of concrete events.

Till about a decade back the birth charts (horoscope) were mostly prepared manually which took a long time. With the availability of computer facility for preparing horoscopes, one can now get a detailed printed horoscope in about 10-15 minutes, showing exact planetary position, different *Varga* charts, *Ashtakavarga,* and *Dasa-Bhukti-Antara* details.

The second step of assessing the potential of the horoscope requires a thorough knowledge of *Karkatwa* (signification) of different houses, the planets posited therein, and benefic or malefic aspect thereon. These details have already been discussed.

After assessing the quality and quantity of result of any house to be experienced by the individual in his life, comes the most important step – WHEN? For this purpose our visionary *Rishis* have given us the tools of *Dasa-Bhukti, Gochar* (transit) and *Ashtakavarga* system.

'Dasa' is the name given to the planetary timing system, with the help of which we can calculate when the good or bad result of planets located in different houses of the horoscope will fructify. The success of an astrologer lies in his ability to correctly apply the *dasa* system and pinpoint the event.

Among the various *Dasa* systems, Maharishi Parasara, father of Indian Astrology has preferred the *Vimshottari Dasa* System

Timing of Events

which is uniformly applicable without any condition. The term '*Vimshottari*' means *Vimsh* = 20 and *Ottari* – over and above 100, that is, 100+20 =120 years, which is taken as span of human life. These 120 years have been allotted among 9 planets in the following order : Ketu – 7 yrs., Venus – 20 yrs., Sun – 6 yrs., Moon – 10 yrs., Mars – 7 yrs., Rahu – 18 yrs., Jupiter – 16 yrs., Saturn – 19 yrs., and Mercury – 17 yrs. Though, no reasoning is now available for such an allotment of years to planets, it has stood the test of time. This *Dasa* system is followed by majority of astrologers.

Vimshottari Dasa system works on the longitude (degree) of Moon at the moment of birth. From Moon's longitude we know the *Nakshatra* (Constellation) occupied by it at birth. There are 27 *Nakshatras* in the 360° Zodiac, with a span of 13° 20' each, and these are equally allotted – 3 each – among 9 planets. From *Nakshatra* we know its lord, and calculate balance of its *Dasa* period at birth. The *Dasas* of other planets follow in fixed order thereafter. The following table shows the degrees of the Zodiac occupied by the 27 *Nakshatras*, their lords and *Dasa in seriatim* for ready reference.

Planet	Nakshatras Ruled	Location in the Zodiac	Dasa period
Ketu	*Aswini*	Aries – 0° to 13°20'	
	Magha	Leo - 0° to 13°20'	7 years
	Moola	Sagitt. - 0° to 13°20'	
Venus	*Bharani*	Aries - 13°20' to 26° 40'	
	Purvaphalguni	Leo - 13°20' to 26° 40'	20 years
	Purvashada	Sagitt. - 13°20' to 26° 40'	
Sun	*Kritika*	Aries - 26° 40' to Taurus 10°	
	U. Phalguni	Leo - 26° 40' to Virgo 10°	6 years
	Uttarashada	Sagitt. - 26° 40' to Capri. 10°	
Moon	*Rohini*	Taurus - 10° to 23° 20'	
	Hasta	Virgo - 10° to 23° 20'	10 years
	Sravana	Capri. - 10° to 23° 20'	
Mars	*Mrigsira*	Taurus - 23° 20' to Gemini 6° 40'	
	Chitra	Virgo - 23° 20' to Libra 6° 40'	7 years
	Dhanishta	Capri. - 23° 20' to Aqua. 6° 40'	
Rahu	*Aridra*	Gemini - 6° 40' to 20°	

	Swati	Libra - 6° 40' to 20°	18 years
	Satabisha	Aqua. - 6° 40' to 20°	
Jupiter	Punarvasu	Gemini - 20° to Cancer 3° 20'	
	Visakha	Libra - 20° to Scorpio 3° 20'	16 years
	P.Bhadrapada	Aqua. - 20° to Pisces 3° 20'	
Saturn	Pushya	Cancer 3° 20' to 16° 40'	
	Anuradha	Scorpio 3° 20' to 16° 40'	19 years
	U. Bhadrapada	Pisces 3° 20' to 16° 40'	
Mercury	Ashlesha	Cancer 16° 40' to 30°	
	Jyeshtha	Scorpio 16° 40' to 30°	17 years
	Revati	Pisces 16° 40' to 30°	
9 Planets	27 Nakshatras	360°	120 years

Suppose the Moon is posited in Leo at 13° 20'. From that degree *Purvaphalguni Nakshatra* starts. This means that Ketu *Dasa* is over and Venus *Dasa* is just starting. There is balance of Venus *Dasa* in full (20 years) at birth, after which the *Dasas* of Sun- 6 yrs., Moon – 10 yrs., Mars – 7 yrs., Rahu – 18 yrs., and so on will follow in fixed cyclic order indicated above.

It may be clarified that it is not always that Moon at birth will be at the exact beginning of a *Nakshatra*. It can occupy any degree from the beginning till the end of a *Nakshatra*. In such cases the balance of the *Nakshatra* lord's *Dasa* at birth is calculated on proportionate basis. As the whole *Nakshatra* (13° 20') covers certain specified years of that lord's *Dasa*, then how many years will be represented by the remaining distance to be covered by the Moon in that *Nakshatra*. Thereafter, the balance of first *Bhukti* in operation in that *Dasa* at birth is arrived at. The first *Bhukti* in every horoscope is not necessarily that of the main *Dasa* lord.

Calculation of *Bhukti* (Sub-period)

In the above example, all the 20 years of Venus *Dasa* cannot give the same result year after year. The change of events is indicated by 9 *Bhuktis* (sub-periods) in each *Dasa*. The total ruling *Dasa* period is proportionately divided into 9 *Bhuktis*, starting from that of *Dasa* lord followed by *Bhuktis* of other planets in the fixed order. In the above example of Venus *Dasa* (20 years) the first *Bhukti* will be of

Timing of Events

Venus itself, followed by that of the Sun, Moon, Mars, Rahu, Jupiter, etc. For calculating the duration of *Bhukti* period of any planet in a particular *Dasa*, we multiply the years of *Dasa* lord with years of *Bhukti* lord *Dasa*. The first digit of the resultant figure from the right multiplied with 3 gives the duration in days. The remaining figure on the left of first digit indicates the period in months. In our example 20 × 20 = 400. Multiplying the first digit 0 with 3 gives only 0 days, and the remaining figure of 40 indicates the months. Hence, the duration of Venus *Bhukti* in Venus *Dasa* is of 3 years – 4 months – 0 days.

Now to get the next *Bhukti* of Sun multiply the *Dasa* years of Venus (20) with the *Bhukti* lord *Dasa* years (Sun – 6) and get 120. Multiplication of first digit 0 with 3 gives only 0. The remaining figure 12 indicates the months. Hence, the *Bhukti* duration of Sun in Venus *Dasa* is 12 months or 1 year – 0 month – 0 days. In this way we can find out *Bhukti* duration of any planet in any *Dasa*.

Calculation of *Antara* (Sub-Sub period)

For further shortening of time period we calculate *Antara* (Sub-Sub period). For this we multiply *Dasa* lord years with that of *Bhukti* lord *Dasa* years and *Dasa* years of *Antara* lord. Then, divide the resultant figure by 40. The final figure indicates the number of days of *Antara*. In our example, to find the duration of Venus *Antara* in Venus *Dasa*-Venus *Bhukti* we proceed as follows: 20 × 20 × 20 = 8000, divided by 40, and we get 200 days or 0 year – 6 months – 20 days. For calculating the *Antara* of Venus-Venus-Sun we multiply 20 × 20 × 6 = 2400, divide by 40, and get 60 days or 2 months. So, Sun *Antara* in Venus *Dasa* – Venus *Bhukti* is of 2 months.

In this way we can calculate the *Bhukti* and *Antara* period in any planet's *Dasa*. In computer made horoscope the exact *Dasa* balance at birth and subsequent *Dasa-Bhukti-Antara* details are readily available.

Judgment of *Dasa* Result

Lagna is the fulcrum of the horoscope. When *Lagna* is strong and its lord is also strong (being exalted, *Vargottam*, in *Mooltrikona* or own sign or associated with or aspected by benefic planets) the person leads a comfortable life. If *Lagna* contains weak or malefic planets and *Lagna* lord is also weak or afflicted, the individual faces troubles in life.

All planets when located in own sign, own *Navamsa*, in exaltation, in *Mooltrikona*, in *Kendra* from *Lagna* give good result in their *Dasa* and *Bhukti*, while the planets which occupy inimical, or debilitation sign, or eclipsed or own 6th, 8th or 12th houses, or in last degree of a sign, give bad result.

A planet during its *Dasa* period gives result according to its inherent nature, the house it occupies and owns, modified by the influence of other planets on it. The result is good or bad depending on the nature and strength of the *Dasa* lord.

According to their *Karkatwa* (natural signification) the *Dasa* result of planets are as follows:-

(1) **Sun**-Strong and unafflicted Sun gives status, wealth, success, fame and happiness. But weak or afflicted Sun gives disease, mental anguish, loss of wealth, and humiliation.

(2) **Moon**-*Pakshbali* and well aspected Moon gives happiness, health, good food, success in business, aquistion of land, cattle, wealth, ornaments and good clothes. During weak or afflicted Moon *Dasa* the above factors become source of worry and unhappiness.

(3) **Mars**-During the *Dasa* of strong and well aspected Mars one gains through bravery, disputes and even cheating. When Mars is weak or afflicted, the individual suffers injury, fever, loss, quarrels with relations, and feels miserable.

(4) **Mercury**-During the *Dasa* of strong and well aspected Mercury, one acquires knowledge and wealth, enjoys comforts, reputation and happiness of wife, children and friends. But a weak or afflicted Mercury causes opposite result in above matters, and the native suffers from many diseases.

(5) **Jupiter**-During the *Dasa* of strong and well associated Jupiter one acquires knowledge, wealth and recognition, performs

religious deeds, enjoys company of wife, children and friends, and his desires are fulfilled. But a weak, ill-posited or afflicted Jupiter causes unhappiness on above account, suffering from disease of ear, and phlegm disorders.

(6) **Venus**-During the *Dasa* of strong and well associated Venus, there is material prosperity, acquisition of vehicles, dresses and ornaments. The native enjoys company of young ladies and receives honour from State. But a weak and afflicted Venus disappoints, causes depression and sex related diseases.

(7) **Saturn**-During the *Dasa* of strong and well associated Saturn one attains honour, status and property. But an afflicted Saturn in its *Dasa* gives chronic diseases, desertion by servants, loss of land, happiness and wealth.

(8) **Rahu**-When posited in good house and conjoined with benefics, Rahu gives affluence during its *Dasa* and fulfils all worldly desires. An inauspicious Rahu gives trouble from thieves, cheating, poisonous substances, insult, failure of business and profession and causes worries.

(9) **Ketu**-When well aspected and associated with benefics, Ketu gives religious bent of mind, fame and recognition. An afflicted Ketu causes injuries, diseases, danger from fire, defame, loss of health and wealth.

House Lordship Result

During the *Dasa* of strong *Lagna* lord, the native enjoys good health, prosperity and fame. But during weak, badly posited or afflicted *Lagna* lord *Dasa* the native suffers from fear, disease, mental anxiety, loss of position and other misfortunes.

During the *Dasa* of strong 2nd house lord, the native gets success, good meals, acquisition to family, and income through speech. But during the *Dasa* of badly placed 2nd house lord, he behaves foolishly, receives bad news, suffers from eye trouble and wastes money.

During the *Dasa* of strong 3rd house lord, the native receives help from brothers, gets good news, success in his efforts, and gets appreciation. But during the *Dasa* of badly placed 3rd lord, he faces differences with brothers, failure of his enterprise and humiliations.

During the *Dasa* of strong 4th house lord, the native acquires land, vehicles, new house, wealth, affection of relatives and higher status. But the *dasa* of weak or afflicted 4th house lord gives distress to mother, sickness of relatives, loss of land, property, cattle and status.

During the *dasa* of strong 5th house lord, the native gets recognition, higher status, and happiness of progeny. But during the *Dasa* of weak or afflicted 5th lord, the native suffers from mental aberrations, stomach ailments, sickness to children and faces wrath of Government.

During the *Dasa* of strong 6th house lord, the native enjoys good health, destroys his enemies, becomes powerful and affluent. But the *dasa* of weak or afflicted 6th lord causes reverses, defeat, theft and disease. The native performs evil deeds and gets defame.

During the *Dasa* of strong 7th house lord, one enjoys life with his wife, goes on pleasure trips and acquires new clothes and jewels. But in the *Dasa* of weak or afflicted 7th lord, there is separation from wife, disease of private parts and aimless travels.

During the *Dasa* of strong 8th house lord, the native is free from debts and disputes, there is personal elevation and acquisition of wealth. But during the *Dasa* of weak or afflicted 8th lord, the native suffers from poverty, sickness, humiliation and even death.

During the *Dasa* of strong 9th house lord, the native enjoys happiness, wealth and prosperity. He acts in noble ways and gets State favour. But during the *Dasa* of weak or afflicted 9th lord, one indulges in bad deeds, suffers loss, his wife and children suffer, and a senior member of family may pass away.

During the *Dasa* of strong 10th house lord, one gets higher status, leads a happy life, enjoys fame and success in his enterprise. But during the *Dasa* of weak or afflicted 10th lord, one engages in fruitless enterprises, suffers loss of honour, faces unfortunate events and leads a miserable life.

During the *dasa* of strong *11th* house lord, the native gets regular flow of income, domestic happiness, success and affluence. But during the *dasa* of weak or afflicted 11th lord, the income of the native is reduced, there is trouble to elder brother, sickness of children and he himself suffers from deception and ear ailments.

During the *Dasa* of strong *12th* house lord, the native spends for good cause, performs noble deeds and may earn State honour. But during the *Dasa* of weak or afflicted 12th lord, the native suffers from disease, bondage and dishonour, and his wealth dwindles fast.

A planet in exaltation, *Vargottam*, own or friendly sign produces good result in its *Dasa*, provided its position is not reversed in *Navamsa*, in which case the second half of the *Dasa* is disappointing.

A planet debilitated, *Asta* or in inimical sign or *Trika* (6, 8, 12) houses from Ascendant is considered ill-posited and causes harm in its *Dasa*. If its position is better in *Navamsa,* the second half of the *Dasa* is good.

An exalted planet in birth chart gives recognition, fame, and wealth during its *Dasa*. A benefic retrograde planet produces result like that of an exalted planet, even if it is posited in an inimical or debilitation sign. A *Vargottam* planet gives result like that in *Mooltrikona*. A *Vargottam* but *Asta* or debilitated planet gives mixed result. The *Dasa* of a planet in own sign in birth chart confers success, honour, house, land with own effort or with the help of a wealthy person. In the *Dasa* of a planet occupying friendly sign the person gains success through his friends, makes new friends, becomes rich and enjoys happiness with his wife and children. The *Dasa* of a planet on the last degree of a *Rasi* gives ailments, trouble, agony or disaster, according to the maleficence acquired by it.

A planet occupying an inimical sign makes the person dependent on others for his living, faces troubles, and even his close friends become enemy. A debilitated planet in its *Dasa* causes loss of position, humiliation and debts. The individual lives in unhealthy places and performs evil deeds. The planet in a neutral sign does not produce any worthwhile effect. An *Asta* planet during its *Dasa* causes loss of health, wealth, wife and children. The *Dasa* of a weak associate of Rahu puts the native through several misfortunes.

The *Dasa* of a benefic or malefic planet owning a *Kendra* (4th, 7th, 10th) gives neutral result. The *Dsasa* of all the planets (benefic or malefic) being lord of *Trines* (1st, 5th, 9th) is auspicious. The *Dasa* of lord 3rd, 6th and 11th houses, even if benefic, proves inauspicious.

The planet owning 8th house or posited in 8th house causes much problem during its *Dasa*, and if weak may even cause demise of the individual. But the *Dasa* of 8th lord when it also owns *Lagna* will prove favourable. The blemish of 8th house lordship does not apply to Lagna lord, the Sun and the Moon.

When the lord of *Trikona* occupies a *Kendra*, or vice-versa, its *Dasa* gives auspicious result. These planets cooperate to produce the most auspicious result in their *Bhukti* in each other's *Dasa*.

The lords of a *Kendra* and *Trikona* house, if owner of a bad house, by their relationship form *Yoga* and give some good result.

A *Trikona* lord in its *Bhukti* in the *Dasa* of a *Kendra* lord, and vice-versa, gives good result even though the two are not in any way related.

When the lord of a *Kendra* is conjoined with the lord of *Trikona*, both become powerful to increase prosperity. If there is association of another *Trikona* lord, the prosperity is manifold.

Jupiter and Venus as lords of *Kendra*, except *Lagna*, cause harm. If these are also located in *Maraksthan* (2nd and 7th houses), these become powerful to cause death during their *Dasa*. Mercury as lord of *Kendra* is less harmful than Jupiter and Venus, while Moon is the least harmful.

The *Dasa* of a benefic planet will be auspicious when it also conjoins with, or is aspected by, a benefic planet.

When benefic planets are placed in their depression, or in inimical sign, or in *Trika* (6th, 8th, 12th) house, their *Dasa* gives untoward result, while malefics in similar situation cause misery in their *Dasa*.

When the *Dasa* lord is conjoined with, or aspected by, malefics, its *Dasa* period causes loss of wealth and honour. When the *Dasa* lord is associated with a planet of mixed nature, its *Dasa* and *Bhukti* will produce mixed result. When the *Dasa* lord is associated with an inimical planet, then during its *Dasa* that individual's enemies will increase and the efforts are not fruitful.

A planet debilitated, *Asta* or in *Bhava Sandhi*, is incapable of giving good result, nor is any other planet conjoined with such a planet able to produce any good. A combust planet (*Asta*) behaves as if debilitated.

The *Dasa* of a planet ruling *Sampat* (2nd), *Kshema* (4th) *Sadhak* (6th), *Mitra* (8th) and *Param Mitra* (9th) *Nakshatra* from *Janma Nakshatra* gives prosperity to the native. But during the *Dasa* of a planet ruling *Vipat* (3rd) *Pratyak* (5th) or *Nidhan* (7th) *Nakshatra* from *Janma Nakshatra* the native experiences much distress. Within the *Dasa* of a malefic planet, the *Bhukti* of the lord of *Vipat*, *Pratyak* and *Vadha Tara* gives grief or injury.

When at the start of its *Dasa* a planet happens to be in its exaltation, own or friendly sign, or in an *Upachaya* (3, 6, 10 or 11) houses from *Lagna*, or receives the aspect of a benefic or friendly planet, its *Dasa* and *Bhukti* gives good result.

When at the start of a planet's *Dasa*, *Pakshbali* Moon transits the exaltation, own or friendly sign of the *Dasa* lord, or is in an *Upachaya*, *Trikona* or 7th house from the *Dasa* lord, the result is happy.

In the *Dasa* of a benefic planet, the effect of the house it owns is experienced at the beginning of the *Dasa*; while the result by virtue of its positional strength (exaltation/own sign, etc.) will manifest in the middle of the *Dasa*, and the result of the aspect of other planets on it, is experienced towards the end.

In the case of a malefic planet, the effect of its positional strength (exaltation, own sign, etc.) will be felt first. The *Bhava* lordship result will be experienced in the middle, while the result of aspecting planet will be felt towards the end of the *Dasa*. These details are tabulated below for easy rememberance.

	Benefic Planet *Dasa*	Malefic Planet *Dasa*
At first :	Result of *Bhava* owned	Positional strength result.
Middle :	Positional strength result.	Result of *Bhava* owned.
The end :	Aspect result.	Aspect result

In the sequence of *Dasas*, if the 4th *Dasa* belongs to Saturn, the 5th *Dasa* to Mars or Rahu, the 6th *Dasa* to Jupiter, these prove problematic and dangerous.

Judgment of *Bhukti* Result

The planets do not give their full (good or bad) result during their own *Bhukti*. It is during the *Bhuktis* of other planets related to *Dasa* lord that such result is experienced.

The characteristics (good or bad) of *Bhukti* lord influences the main *Dasa* lord. If *Bhukti* lord is a benefic and occupies good house (other than 6th, 8th or 12th), or own *Navamsa*, it gives very good result, while a malefic *Bhukti* lord adversely affects the result of *Mahadasa* lord. When the *Bhukti* lord directly casts its influence on *Dasa* lord by conjunction or aspect, the *Bhukti* lord result is prominently felt.

Whichever house reckoned from the *Mahadasa* lord is occupied by the *Bhukti* lord, it is only the result of the house from *Lagna* that comes to pass during *Bhukti* period.

During the *Dasa* and *Bhukti* of benefic planets, the native gets position, wealth and conveyance. During the *Dasa* of a malefic planet and *Bhukti* of a benefic planet the native first gets good result followed by bad result. During the *Dasa* of a benefic and *Bhukti* of malefic planet, the individual faces trouble first and then happy events. Evil result should be declared during *Bhukti* period when *Bhukti* lord is posited in *Trika* (6th, 8th or 12th) house, and it is not located in its exaltation, *Mooltrikona*, own or friendly sign.

House – wise result of *Dasa* and *Bhukti*

During the *Dasa* of *Lagna* lord and *Bhukti* of a benefic and friendly planet, the person experiences good health, all round success, and happiness. However, during the *Bhukti* of a malefic planet or unfriendly to *Mahadasa* lord, or located in 6th, 8th or 12th house, or unfriendly to the *Lagna* (Ascendant), the individual faces loss, disease, distress and danger from enemies. If the *Lagna* lord is weak but located in *Kendra* or *Trikona*, the suffering is less.

If a malefic planet occupies *Lagna*, then during its *Dasa* and in the *Bhukti* of a malefic planet there will be much distress, disease, loss of wealth and danger from enemies. The effect will be mixed in the *Bhukti* of a benefic planet.

During the *Dasa* of benefic lord of 2nd house and the *Bhukti* of a benefic planet there will be gain of wealth and happiness from family.

If the lord of 2nd house is malefic, then there will be loss of wealth, eye or face disease during the *Bhukti* of Saturn, Mars, Rahu and the Sun.

When a malefic planet occupies the 2nd house, during the *Bhukti* of that planet the person concerned gets punishment from Government, suffers loss of honour, wealth and status, and differences with friends and relatives.

During the *Dasa* of a benefic lord of 3rd house and the *Bhukti* of another benefic planet, the person succeeds in his efforts, gains recognition, and has good relations with his younger siblings.

But during the *Dasa* of malefic lord of 3rd house and the *Bhukti* of Saturn, Mars, Rahu, Ketu and the Sun, irrespective of their location, there are serious differences with younger brother/sister or even their loss.

During the *Dasa* of lord of 4th house and the *Bhukti* of a benefic and strong planet, there will be gain of wealth, land, house, cattle, conveyance, comfort and happiness. However, in the *Bhukti* of a weak malefic planet there will be quarrel with relations, damage to agriculture, cattle and wealth.

During the *Dasa* of 4th house lord and *Bhukti* of Saturn, Rahu, Mars and the Sun there is change of residence. Similar result follows during the *Bhukti* of a debilitated or *Asta* planet.

During the *Dasa* of lord of 5th house and *Bhukti* of a benefic planet, there will be acquisition of wealth and children, recognition from State and fulfilment of desires. But when *Bhukti* lord is malefic planet there is confusion of intellect, disease from bad food, defame and disease to children.

During the *Dasa* of strong 6th lord one enjoys good health, destruction of enemies, gain of power and wealth. But during the *Dasa* of the 6th house and *Bhukti* of a malefic planet, the individual suffers through Government, thieves, debts and disease.

During the *Dasa* of benefic lord of 7th house and *Bhukti* of a benefic planet, the native enjoys conjugal bliss and prosperity. But during the *Dasa* of malefic lord of 7th house and *Bhukti* of a malefic planet, there is opposition from wife, or her separation, sexual diseases, unfruitful foreign travel, and also wrath of Government.

During the *Dasa* of 8th lord and in the *Bhukti* of a malefic planet (Rahu, Mars, or Saturn) there is danger to life, wealth, status and honour and loss of wife.

During the *Dasa* of the lord of 9th house, the native enjoys good time, happiness and wealth, but during the *Bhukti* of a malefic planet (Saturn, Mars or Rahu), the native has set back in career, there is harm to parents and waste of wealth.

During the *Dasa* of strong 10th lord one enjoys success, fame, rise in status and happiness. But in the *Bhukti* of a malefic planet, family member may fall sick, there may be loss of office, status, wealth and reputation.

During the *Dasa* of strong lord of 11th house, there is smooth flow of income, domestic happiness, affluence and success in efforts. However, during the malefic *Bhukti* of Saturn, Mars, Rahu or Sun, there is ruin of cultivation and other operations, ear ailments, sorrow, fall in income, and trouble to children and elder brother.

During the *Dasa* of strong 12th lord there is expenditure on noble cause. However, in the *Bhukti* of Saturn, Mars or Rahu, the person suffers from grief, differences with his wife, sons, and suffers loss of honour and wealth. During the *Bhukti* of Rahu (*Karka* for poison) the individual may be exposed to danger from poison.

During the *Bhukti* of planets which are located in the 6th, or 8th house from *Lagna* or *Dasa* lord, the individual faces untoward result about the houses where these are posited and rule over, in the form of unfavourable State action, opposition from wife and subordinates, trouble from thieves, fire, relatives, unhappiness and diseases.

During the *Bhukti* of a malefic planet located in the 12th house from the Main *Dasa* lord, the native loses his position, faces opposition from relatives, friends, trouble in feet or eyes and goes abroad.

During the *Bhukti* of a benefic planet located in 2nd house from Main *Dasa* lord, the native enjoys happiness, good food, clothes and help from others.

Thus the *Bhukti* lord influences the *Mahadasa* result for good or bad according to the basic nature and relationship with *Dasa* lord. In this connection we may take practical hint from *Jatak Parijat* which states the result of Saturn *Bhukti* in the *Dasa* of Jupiter as follows:

द्वेषबुद्धि मनस्तापं पुत्रमूलाद्धनव्ययम्।
कर्मनाशमवाप्नोति शनौ जीवदशान्तरे।

(Ch. 18, Sl. 112)

meaning, "There will be a feeling of aversion, mental anguish and waste of wealth through son and failure of business." Here *Bhukti* lord malefic Saturn influences the result of *Dasa* lord Jupiter who is significator for son and wealth, resulting in mental anguish due to loss.

Then about the result of Mercury *Bhukti* in Jupiter *Dasa*, *Jatak Parijat* states:

वैश्यवर्गेण वित्ताप्तिं राजस्नेहं सुखवहम्
सत्कर्माच रसिद्धिं च बुधेजीवदशान्तरे।।

(Ch. 18, Sl. 113)

meaning, "The individual acquires wealth from trading community, gets royal favour, material comforts, and performs good deeds." Here, Mercury augments the benefic result of *Dasa* lord Jupiter.

Mutual *Dasa – Bhukti* of Saturn and Venus reshuffles the native's life. The mutual *Dasa-Bhukti* of Venus and Jupiter causes trouble from family members. The mutual *Dasa – Bhukti* of Saturn and Sun ensures success when both the planets are strong in *Rasi* placement. When either of these is adversely placed, the period leads to grief. Mutual *Dasa – Bhukti* of weak Jupiter and Mars gives trouble from progeny and wife. During the mutual *Dasa – Bhukti* of Saturn and Rahu the native suffers neurological disorders, when any two of the *Lagna*, Sun, Moon or 2nd house, are in any way associated with Saturn or Rahu. The mutual *Dasa – Bhukti* of Rahu and Ketu gives troubles, disease or accident coupled with severe anxiety. Towards the end of a *Dasa* (in last *Bhukti*) the result already in operation turns adverse. This period is known as *Dasa-Chidra*.

Antara Lord has the Final Say

Every planet has its unique characteristics which fructify during the *Dasa*, *Bhukti* and *Antara* period. The planets produce their general features based on their strength in the horoscope during the entire life of the individual in the form of social status and temperament. The planets bring forth their specific result during their *Dasa* according to their location and strength in the natal horoscope. These influence the physical features, temperament, as well as the individual's social and family status. The general fortune of the individual varies according to the change of *Bhukti* in the main *Dasa* of planet.

Every planet in its *Mahadasa* accommodates the distinctive features of other planets during their *Bhukti* period, thereby producing new situations for the individual. The *Bhukti* lord produces concrete result and *Antara lord* fructifies the actual result.

The actualization of an event depends upon the nature, disposition and strength of the *Antara* lord. Unless the *Antara* lord is strong and favourable, good effect of benefic planet at the *Dasa – Bhukti* level cannot fructify.

Rules for Judging Rahu/Ketu *Dasa*

Rahu gives good or bad result depending upon the nature of the planet it associates with. A planet, though good and benefic by itself,

Timing of Events

due to its association with Rahu will cause malefic effect during the end of its *Dasa*.

When Rahu or Ketu occupies a house belonging to a benefic planet, and is not connected with any planet, it produces good result in its own *Bhukti* in the *Mahadasa* of the lord of the benefic house occupied by it.

When Rahu or Ketu has no connection but occupies a *Kendra* or *Trikona* house, in that case the *Bhukti* of a *Yoga karka* planet during its (Rahu/Ketu) *Dasa* gives good result.

During *Dasa* of the dispositor of Rahu or Ketu, the native may face excessive troubles, accident or disease when it is conjunct with malefics or is located in an adverse house.

Rahu or Ketu in houses 6, 8, 12 associated with benevolent planets can give rise to the same effects during its relevant *Dasa* or *Bhukti*.

Mutual *Dasa* and *Bhukti* of Rahu and Ketu or the above mentioned planets, also causes troubles, disease, accident or excessive anxiety.

Transit

The horoscope indicates the exact location of the constantly moving planets at the time of birth of a person. Their future movement is called *Gochar* (Transit), and helps in arriving at the actual events in one's life. The rules for judgment of transit result of planets are different from that of the planets in natal chart. Transit result of planets is primarily judged with reference to their location from Moon at birth. It is considered advisable to look it up from *Lagna*, the Sun and the house under consideration as well for certainty of prediction.

The time taken by different planets to transit through a sign is as follows:

Sun	30 days	Moon	- 2 ½ days
Mars	45 days	Mercury	- 21 days
Venus	27 days	Jupiter	- about 390 days
Rahu/Keru	540 days	Saturn	- about 900 days.

The transit of Saturn, Rahu, Jupiter, Mars and the Sun is the most useful for predictive purpose. Due to their longer stay in a sign the transit of Jupiter, Rahu and Saturn has lasting influence on the individual.

The Sun and Mars give their result while transitting through the first 10° of the sign. Jupiter and Venus give their result when transitting between 10° to 20°. The Moon and Saturn give their result when transitting between 20° to 30°. Mercury, Rahu and Ketu give their result throughout their transit in a sign.

The planets give indication of their expected result during transit through the next house as follows:

The Sun	- 5 days before	Mercury	- 7 days before
Mars	- 8 days before	Moon	- 3 *Ghatis* before. (2½ *Ghatis* = one hour)
Jupiter	- 2 months before	Saturn	- 6 months before.
Rahu/Ketu	- 3 months before		

After deciding the favourable *Dasa-Bhukti* for any event, we look up favourable transit of Saturn and Rahu; come to year through favourable transit of Jupiter; to month by looking at the favourable transit of the Sun; and reach approximate day by Moon's favourable transit.

Each planet produces favourable result during transit through certain houses counted from Moon, and unfavourable result during transit through the rest. All the planets give good result while transiting through 11th house from Moon. Only Venus gives good result while transitting through 12th house from Moon. Occasionally, the transit effect is blocked by the presence of other planets vis-à-vis the transiting planet. This is called '*Vedha*' (obstruction). The benefic result of transiting planet fructifies when there is no '*Vedha*'. Saturn and the Sun, and Mercury and the Moon, do not have mutual '*Vedha*' The benefic transit of planets through different houses from Moon and their *Vedha* position is as under.

Timing of Events

Planets	Favourable transit from Moon / Vedha position							
Sun	$\frac{3^{rd}}{9^{th}}$,	$\frac{6^{th}}{12^{th}}$,	$\frac{10^{th}}{4^{th}}$,	$\frac{11^{th}}{5^{th}}$ Saturn here does not cause *Vedha*.				
Moon	$\frac{1^{st}}{5^{th}}$	$\frac{3^{rd}}{9^{th}}$	$\frac{6^{th}}{12^{th}}$	$\frac{7^{th}}{2^{nd}}$	$\frac{10^{th}}{4^{th}}$,	$\frac{11^{th}}{8^{th}}$ Mercury here does not cause *Vedha*.		
Mars	$\frac{3^{rd}}{12^{th}}$	$\frac{6^{th}}{9^{th}}$	$\frac{11^{th}}{5^{th}}$					
Jupiter	$\frac{2^{nd}}{12^{th}}$	$\frac{5^{th}}{4^{th}}$	$\frac{7^{th}}{3^{rd}}$	$\frac{9^{th}}{10^{th}}$	$\frac{11^{th}}{8^{th}}$			
Saturn	$\frac{3^{rd}}{12^{th}}$	$\frac{6^{th}}{9^{th}}$	$\frac{11^{th}}{5^{th}}$ Sun here does not cause *Vedha*.					
Mercury	$\frac{2^{nd}}{5^{th}}$	$\frac{4^{th}}{3^{rd}}$	$\frac{6^{th}}{9^{th}}$	$\frac{8^{th}}{1^{st}}$	$\frac{10^{th}}{8^{th}}$	$\frac{11^{th}}{12^{th}}$ Moon here doesnot cause *Vedha*.		
Venus	$\frac{1^{st}}{8^{th}}$	$\frac{2^{nd}}{7^{th}}$	$\frac{3^{rd}}{1^{st}}$	$\frac{4^{th}}{10^{th}}$	$\frac{5^{th}}{9^{th}}$	$\frac{8^{th}}{5^{th}}$	$\frac{9^{th}}{11^{th}}$	$\frac{11^{th}}{3^{rd}}$	$\frac{12^{th}}{6^{th}}$
Rahu/Ketu	$\frac{3^{rd}}{12^{th}}$	$\frac{6^{th}}{9^{th}}$	$\frac{11^{th}}{5^{th}}$					

To understand the above chart, let us take Sun's transit. Sun produces good result while transiting through 3rd, 6th, 10th and 11th houses from Moon. In *3rd house,* the Sun gives health, wealth and status, which will remain under check so long as there is a planet in 9th from Moon, except Saturn. In *6th house,* the Sun removes diseases, enemies and sorrows. The effect will remain under check so long as a planet, other than Saturn, transits through 12th house from Moon. In *10th house,* the Sun gives higher status, promotion and success in enterprise. This effect will remain under check so long as a planet, other than Saturn, transits through 4th house from Moon. Sun's transit through 11th house confers wealth, success and freedom from sickness. This effect remains withheld so long as a planet, other than Saturn, transits through 5th house from the Moon.

The transit of Sun through other houses spoils that house matters as follows:

1st house - Health and wealth.

2nd house - Wealth and eyes.

4th house - Happiness and peace of mind.

5th house - Causes mental agitation and embarrassment.

7th house - Causes stomach problem, humiliation and tiring journeys.

8th house - Causes obstacles, fear, illness and displeasure of authorities.

9th house - Causes humiliation, separation from relatives and depression.

12th house - Causes sorrow, loss of wealth, quarrel with friends and illness.

Similarly, result of transit of other planets may be analysed.

This two – fold analysis of planetary position – at birth and current transit is helpful in correct delineation of actual events in an individual's life. The planetary position in the horoscope at birth indicates the inherent potential. The favourable *Dasa – Bhukti* coupled with favourable transit materializes the potential of the horoscope.

Transit of *Dasa* Lord

When a planet whose *Dasa* is operating, is strong in birth chart and transits through its exaltation, own or friendly sign, it promotes the prosperity of the house (s) it represents, reckoned from *Lagna*.

When the *Dasa* lord in transit passes through the *Lagna*, 3rd, 6th, 10th or 11th houses from *Lagna*, or when a friendly or benefic planet comes to *Lagna*, the *Dasa* result becomes favourable.

When the *Dasa* of a weak or debilitated or eclipsed (*Asta*) planet in natal chart is in operation, it destroys the matters of the houses it transits.

Transit of *Bhukti* Lord

When the *Bhukti* lord during transit passes through own, or exaltation sign, or be retrograde, the result will be favourable. But when the *Bhukti* lord during transit is debilitated, in inimical sign or becomes eclipsed by the Sun, the native suffers.

The good result of a planet whose *Bhukti* is auspicious will fructify when the Sun transits through the exaltation sign of that planet.

Similar benefic result will be experienced when Jupiter transits through the exaltation sign of the *Bhukti* lord.

When the Moon transits through a house which happens to be the exaltation sign of the *Dasa* lord, or its friendly sign, *Upachaya* (3rd, 6th, 10th or 11th) houses, a *Trikona* or the 7th house with respect to the *Mahadasa* lord, the result is favourable. It is untoward when the Moon transits through the remaining places.

The planet whose *Bhukti* is inauspicious, the evil effect will be felt when the Sun transits over the debilitation or inimical sign of the *Bhukti* lord.

Importance of Saturn's Transit

Saturn is *Karak* (significator) for misery, poverty and sorrow, which makes it the most dreaded planet. The duration of Saturn's *Dasa* is 19 years. It takes the longest time (about 2½ years) to transit through a sign/house and has lasting influence on the native.

As explained earlier, Saturn gives good result while transiting through the 3rd, 6th and 11th houses from natal Moon in the horoscope. During Saturn's benefic transit the individual achieves success, gains in status, gets freedom from disease, increased income, and the individual enjoys material prosperity.

Among the remaining 22½ years, Saturn's transit through 12th house to Moon, over Moon, and in 2nd house to the Moon (the period of 7½ years) is called *Sade-sati*. This period is problematic when Saturn is unfavourable to *Lagna*, and Moon is weak or afflicted or lord of 6th, 8th or 12th houses. In addition, Saturn's transit through the 4th, 7th and 8th houses from Moon's location is also problematic and this transit is called *Dhaiya* (malefic 2½ years).

The result of Saturn's transit during *Sade-sati* and *Dhaiya* are as follows.

Through 12th to Moon :	It produces disease, loss of money, destruction of property, theft and other frustrating experiences. Unless the individual is spiritually inclined, there is danger of moral lapse.
Over the Moon :	It causes depression, fatigue, loss of wealth, lack of enthusiasm, humiliation, social and financial tension, and denial of opportunities for growth and material prosperity.
2nd to Moon :	The family harmony is disturbed and there is loss of assets. The person remains away from family. But this transit is helpful for spiritual progress.
4th to Moon :	This transit disturbs emotions, peace of mind, official career and married life. Those psychologically weak suffer the most.
7th to Moon :	The native moves from place to place without respite. He has differences with his wife and business partner, and faces their non-cooperation. The native is confused and suffers from inferiority complex.
8th to Moon :	The native suffers loss of money and separation from near and dear ones. He faces public ridicule, family disturbances, loss in speculation and problem to children. The individual suffers patiently. But this period is good for spiritual progress.

The transit result of Saturn through the remaining houses from the Moon is as follows:

5th to Moon :	The wealth of the individual declines, his children suffer, family members desert him and his career is disturbed. The individual

	feels frustrated, becomes introvert and anti-social. He gets spiritual awakening.
9th to Moon	: The individual loses money and support from elders, and there is death of one of his elders. It is a period of great uncertainty.
10th to Moon	: There is loss of honour, physical discomfort, disturbed life, fall from status, estrangement with his wife, change of residence and environment. There is diversion in his thinking from materialism to spiritualism.

When an individual faces adverse transit of Saturn during the *Mahadasa* of Saturn or Rahu, it is quite problematic. When two or three members of the family have *Sade-sati* in operation, that period is the most trying period of life for the family. The individual feels abandoned, and forsaken by one and all. He does not receive any help from any quarter. This experience develops his fortitude and unfolds his inner strength. Saturn removes the materialistic veil over his inner eyes and inclines him to spiritualism. The favourable transit of benefic Jupiter gives some respite. Saturn as *Lagna* lord for Capricorn and Aquarius *Lagna* born, and as *Yoga karka* for Taurus and Libra *Lagna* born, does not give much problem during *Sade-sati*. It is also kind to Sagittarius and Pisces born persons.

Saturn is the *'Judge of human actions'*. His adverse location in the horoscope indicates that the individual had done some related evil in his previous birth and is facing its result in this life. Saturn is harsh on now non-religious and dishonest persons. When Saturn is not favourable in the horoscope, and the individual is facing its malefic transit, he should maintain good conduct, help the poor and down-trodden, and pray to God with a sense of repentance, which makes the problems bearable.

Ashtakavarga

Ashtakavarga is another method for judging the transit result of a planet. It is, in fact, a more refined form of transit, and clearly indicates the result of a planet while transitting through different houses of the horoscope. In this system benefic dots in each house in *Lagna* Chart are calculated from 8 places (*Lagna* and 7 planets, except Rahu and Ketu). A planet can have maximum 8 benefic dots in a house. This chart is called *Bhinna Ashtakavarga* (BAV). If a planet does not have more than 50% of maximum benefic dots. i.e., 4 in a house in BAV Chart, it becomes incapable of good result inspite of being exalted, in *Mooltrikona* or own sign in *Lagna* Chart. The benefic result is commensurate with the number of benefic dots (5 to 8) in a house. Five or more dots in *Lagna*, 2nd, 3rd, 4th, 5th, 9th, 10th and 11th houses make the life of the individual happy. The benefic dots should be less in 6th, 8th and 12th houses. More benefic dots in 7th house are not considered good. The elaborate and time consuming calculation of benefic dots has become easy through the use of computer programmes.

When a planet is strong in the birth chart and transits through a favourable house which has its 5 to 8 benefic dots in BAV Chart, then it gives correspondingly good result of that house matters. With the reduction in the number of favourable dots in house, the strength of the planet to do good correspondingly gets reduced. When the benefic dots are below 4, the planet gives unfavourable result. For example, Sun's transit in 3rd, 6th, 10th and 11th houses from natal Moon gives good result, provided the benefic dots of Sun in these houses are five or more. When the benefic dots in above houses are below 4, the Sun becomes incapable to do good.

When the benefic dots of all planets in each house are added together it is called *Sarvashtakavarga* (SAV). The SAV Chart is used for judging the transit effect of all (benefic or malefic) planets through the 12 houses. The total benefic dots in SAV Chart are 337, and the average number of benefic dots in a house is 28 ($337 \div 12$). The presence of 28 benefic dots in a house in SAV Chart indicates average result of that house matters. When the benefic dots in a house are more than 30, that house becomes significant in an individual's life. More than 30 benefic dots in houses 1, 4 and 11 from *Lagna* makes the native wealthy. 42 benefic dots in a house manifests honour, wealth and good result of that house affairs. Benefic dots between 28 and 30 show mediocre result. Less than 26 benefic dots harm the affairs of that house.

The transit of a benefic or malefic planet through a house having more than 30 benefic dots gives good result. If the transitting planet also has its more than 5 benefic dots in that house, then the result varies from 'very good' to 'excellent'. When the planet's transit is favourable from natal Moon, but in SAV Chart it is medium, then the *Dasa* result is medium. When a planet is weak in transit and SAV benefic dots are also less in that house, then the *Dasa* result at that time is unfavourable.

A planet does not give good result all the time while transiting a house. It gives the best result when it transits through its '*Kaksha*'. Each sign is divided into 8 equal division of 3°45'. These are allotted to planets with respect to their distance from earth. The allocation of '*Kakshas*' is as follows: 1st *Kaksha* – Saturn, 2nd – Jupiter, 3rd – Mars, 4th – Sun, 5th – Venus, 6th – Mercury, 7th – Moon and 8th – *Lagna*. A planet gives its best result while transitting through its *Kaksha* in a house. If the planet in *Lagna* Chart is also located in its own *Kaksha*, then the transit during own *Kaksha* in a house produces the best result.

Ashtakavarga is also helpful in knowing the result of *Dasa-Bhukti* of a planet. In the house that the planet has maximum benefic dots in BAV Chart, good result of that house will be experienced during its *Dasa*. When the transit of *Dasa* lord is also favourable then the individual experiences the best result. The houses in which *Dasa – Bhukti* lords have 6, 7 or 8 benefic dots, the native enjoys good result of those house matters. During *Sade-sati* and *Dhaiya* when Saturn transits through a sign having more own benefic dots, the evil effect is much less.

In this way with the help of *Dasa-Bhukti*, transit and *Ashtakavarga* system we can predict the trends of events in an individual's life.

From *Sarvashtakavarga* we can also judge the relative strength of different houses. Large number of benefic dots in benefic houses indicates that the native leads an above average life. For example, if the number of benefic dots in the 11th house (gain) are more than those in the 10th house (*Karma*), and the dots in the 12th house (expenditure) are less than those in the 11th house, while *Lagna* has sufficiently large number of benefic dots than the 12th house, in that case the individual has good earning, lives a comfortable life and is wealthy. If the number of dots in the 12th house exceed those in the 11th house, the individual is always short of money. If the dots in these places be equal, the life of the individual remains a mixed one, i.e., a mixture of joy and sorrow. When a house is occupied by benefics and also has large number of benefic dots in *Sarvashtakavarga*, the transit of benefics through that produces the most favourable result.

When a wealthy individual does not own a house or he is not able to live in his own house, then his 2nd, 11th, 5th and 9th houses will have large number of benefic dots in SAV Chart but these will be below 25 in 4th house (home), which denies him living in own house.

Ashtakavarga system is an elaborate and composite system of prediction, and all old astrological classics contain a chapter on it. The readers interested in knowing further details may refer to any standard treatise.

Chapter XII
Lucky Births

Everybody in this world cherishes and strives for healthy, wealthy, prosperous and successful life. But only a few lucky ones are able to enjoy these according to their '*Prarabdha*' (result of *Karma* in past life), indicated through planetary position in their horoscope. Out of the hundreds of benefic *Yogas* mentioned in astrological classics, Acharya Varahamihir has selected the following indicators of lucky birth.

शुभं वर्गोत्तमे जन्म वेशिस्थाने च सद्ग्रहे।
अशून्येषु च केन्द्रेषु कारकाख्य ग्रहेषु च।।

(*Brihat Jatak*, Ch.22.4)

meaning, "A native is born lucky if:

(1) Birth *Lagna* is *Vargottam*
(2) Benefic planets are in 2nd to the Sun, forming *Vesi Yoga*.
(3) All the *Kendras* are occupied by planets, and
(4) There are *Karak* planets in the horoscope.

The presence of as many of the above *Yogas* in a horoscope will make the native progressively lucky. It has been observed that in lucky horoscopes there are invariably present other supporting benefic *Yogas*, and the *Dasa* of benefic planets runs during active years (20 to 50 years), which provides a strong base for a prosperous and happy later life.

Let us discuss the above factors in some detail with example horoscopes to appreciate their truth.

1. *Vargottam Lagna*

When the *Lagna* in the birth chart occupies identical sign in *Navamsa Lagna*, it is termed *Vargottam*. (. . . . . वर्गोत्तमास्तत्स्व – नवांशकास्तु।)

The first *Navamsa* of Movable sign (Aries, Cancer, Libra and Capricorn), the 5th *Navamsa* of Fixed sign (Taurus, Leo, Scorpio, Aquarius), and 9th *Navamsa* of Common sign (Gemini, Virgo, Sagittarius and Pisces) are *Vargottam*. According to *Saravali*:

वर्गोत्तमा नवांशस्तथा . . . . सूतौ कुल मुख्यकरा।

(Ch.3.13)

meaning, "The native born in *Vargottam Lagna* becomes an important person in his circle (family)."

Male: DOB: 11.12.1958, 6.00 A.M., Hyderabad.

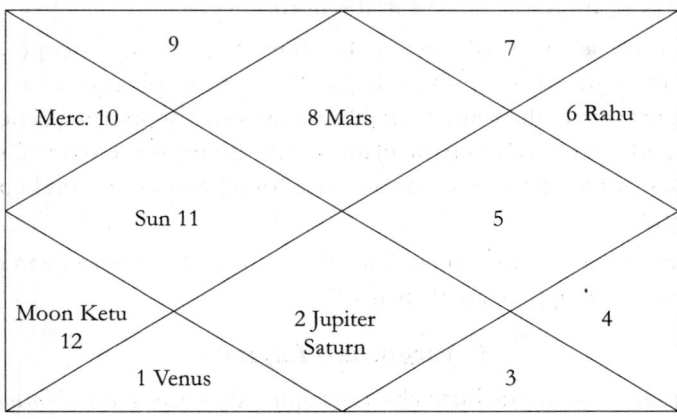

Lagna

Ketu	Mars		
Saturn Venus	*Lagna* Sun Moon Merc.	Jup.	Rahu

Navamsa

Moon Ketu	Venus	Jup. Sat.	
Sun			
Merc.			
	Lagna Mars		Rahu

Lagna is *Vargottam*. In *Lagna* Chart *Lagna* lord Mars aspects *Lagna*, and in *Navamsa* Chart Mars is posited in *Lagna* itself, thereby making *Lagna* exceptionally strong.

The native completed his M. (Tech.) and joined NTPC as Junior Engineer. He completed his Ph.D. during service. He has risen to the rank of Dy. General Manager in less than two decades, and enjoys the reputation of a competent and dedicated officer in the organisation. During Mars *Dasa* he got quick promotions and is due for promotion as Additional General Manager in 2010. The next *Dasa* of *Vargottam* Rahu in Kanya in 11th house will also prove lucky and gainful.

Besides *Vargottam Lagna*, the lords of 9th, 10th and 11th houses are conjoined in *Lagna*, and Rahu and Ketu are also *Vargottam*. Ketu is in 5th house Pisces, and its lord Jupiter is in 12th house. The native is very religious and philanthropic.

2. Vesi Yoga

'*Vesi Yoga*' is formed when there is a planet (other than Moon and Rahu/Ketu) in the 2nd house from the Sun in the birth chart. When benefic planets are located in 2nd to the Sun, it is called *Shubha Vesi Yoga* (*Phaladeepika*, VI.8) and produces very favourable result to the native as follows:

जाता: स्यात् सुभग: सुखी गुणनिधिर्धीरो नृपोधार्मिको।

(Ch. VI. 9)

meaning, "One born in *Shubha Vesi Yoga* is handsome, happy, meritorious, brave, religious and virtuous like a king."

Lucky Births

(1) Dr. S. Radhakrishnan, former President of India.
    DOB: 5.9.1888, 1.30 P.M., at Turitani (T.N.).

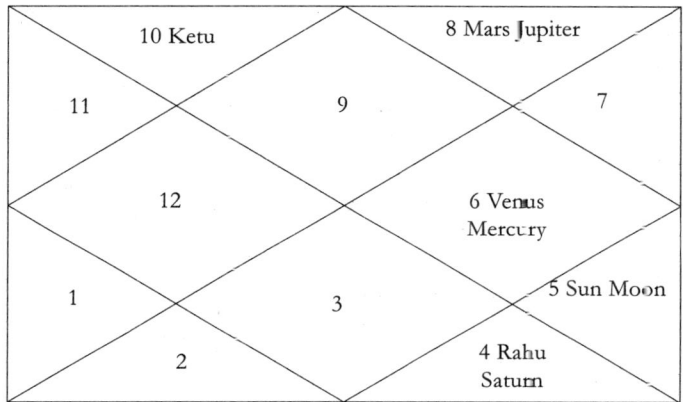

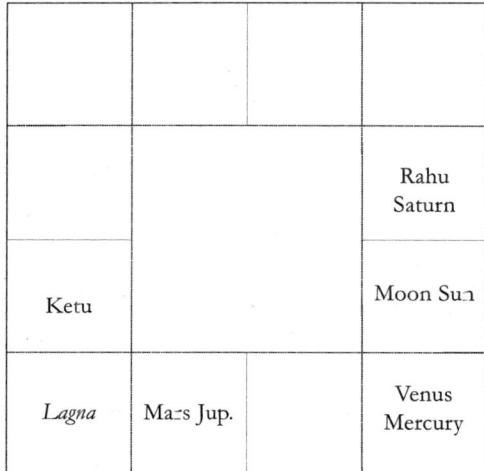

The 9th lord Sun is in 9th house, and exalted Mercury (10th lord in 10th) along with *Neecha Bhanga* Venus in 2nd to the Sun form powerful *Shubha Vesi Yoga*. He was world famous thinker, and Professor of Philosophy and Religion. He was India's Ambassador abroad, Vice-President, and then the President of India.

(2) Dr. B.V. Raman, former Editor of Astrological Magazine, DOB: 8.8.1912, 1915 hrs., Bangalore.

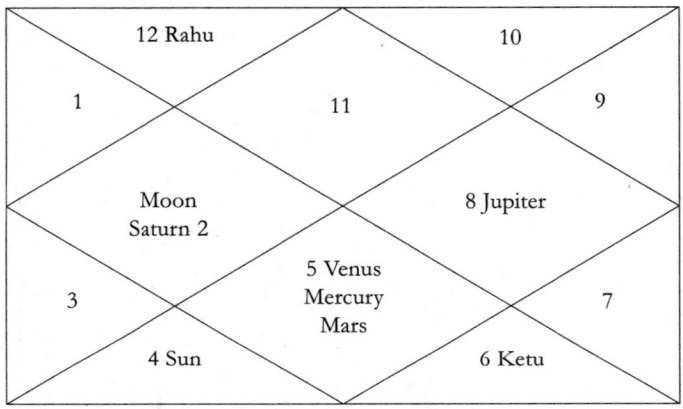

Rahu		Moon Saturn	
Lagna			Sun
			Venus Mercury Mars
	Jupiter		Ketu

Venus, Mercury, and 3rd and 10th lord Mars, are conjoined in Leo in 2nd house to the Sun posited in Cancer. Four benefic and two malefic planets are located in three *Kendras*.

He was world famous Indian astrologer, who revived the publication of the *Astrological Magazine* at a young age and later wrote many books on Astrology.

Lucky Births

Jupiter, Moon sign lord Venus, and *Lagna* lord are in *Kendra* which made him world famous during middle age.

3. Planets in *Kendra*

Kendras are called *Vishnusthan* (house of happiness) and *Trikonas* are called *Lakshmisthan* (house of wealth). The four *Kendras* in the horoscope are like four walls of a building. When all the *Kendras* are occupied by planets it augments the potential of the horoscope. According to *Jatakdeshmarg*:

लग्नकेन्द्र स्थितै: सर्वेयोगो मङ्गलकारक:॥
मङ्गलाख्ये नरो जातं नित्यं कल्याणकारक:।
वाग्मी प्रभावी धीमांश्च दीर्घायुश्चैत विन्दति॥

(Ch. VIII, 29, 41)

meaning, "When all the planets are in *Kendra* from *Lagna*, *Mangal Yoga* is formed. A person born in *Mangal Yoga* is intelligent, influential, good speaker, does good deeds and has long life."

Varahmihir also tells

केन्द्रै: सद्सद्युतैर्दलाख्यौ।
स्त्रकसर्पौ कथितौ पराशरेण॥

(*Brihat Jatak*, Ch. 12.2)

meaning, "Maharishi Parasara speaks of two *Dala Yogas* – '*Sruk*' and '*Sarpa*' – formed by the location of benefics and malefics respectively in *Kendras*." '*Sruk*' Yoga is formed by benefics (Jupiter, Venus, Mercury and waxing Moon) without any malefic planet either with them or singly in other *Kendra*. '*Sruk*' Yoga confers all pleasantaries in life. But when the malefics (Saturn, Mars and the Sun) occupy three *Kendras* without any benefic conjoined with them or in the 4th *Kendra*, it is called '*Sarpa*' Yoga, and produces a sorrowful and miserable life.

(1) Dr. M.S. Subbalakshmi, World Famous Carnatic Singer, DOB: 16.9.1916, 9.30 A.M., Madurai.

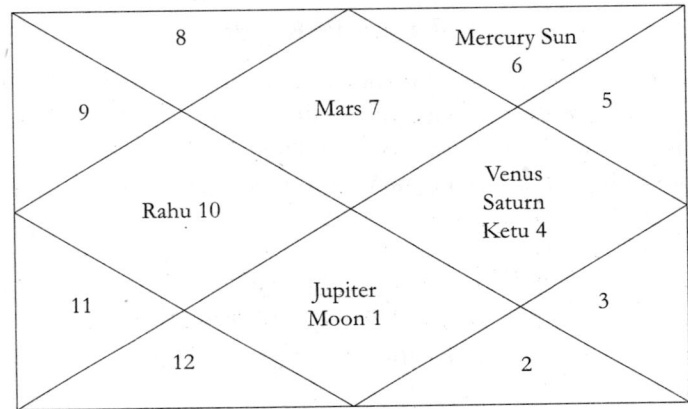

All *Kendras* are filled by planets. Jupiter, Moon, *Lagna* lord Venus, Moon sign lord Mars and *Yoga karka* Saturn are all in *Kendras* and greatly strengthen her horoscope. She was famous Carnatic classical singer. She performed at the U.N. General Assembly and gave concerts at all the famous cities of the world. In recognition of her merit she was conferred *Bharat Ratna* Award in 1986. She earned huge amounts from her concerts, but gave it away in charity, as the 9th lord Mercury

Lucky Births

and 11ᵗʰ lord Sun are in 12ᵗʰ house aspected by Saturn. She lived a long life of 88 years and was accorded a State funeral.

Jatakadeshmarg mentions another lucky *Yoga* as under:

केन्द्रत्रिकोणगा: सर्वेतिष्ठन्ति यदि खेचर:।
य:कश्चित्स्वोच्च राशिस्थो योग: स्याच्छङ्ख ईरित:॥
शङ्खयोगोद्भवो मर्त्यो राजा वा तत्समोऽपि वा।
देवतातद्भंगयुक्तो दाने नृप समो भवेत्॥

(Ch. VIII, Sl. 65-66)

meaning, "When all the planets are in *Kendra* and *Trikona* and one of them is in exaltation, then *Sankha Yoga* is formed. An individual born with *Sankha Yoga* becomes prosperous like a king, enjoys all comforts like *Devatas*, and is also charitable like a king."

Varahamhir also tells:

मध्ये वयस: सुखप्रदा केन्द्रस्था गुरूजन्मलग्नपा:।

(*Erihat Jatak*, 22.5)

meaning "In a horoscope when Jupiter, Moon sign lord, and *Lagna* lord – all the three – are in *Kendra*, then that native enjoys happiness in middle age."

(2) Shri Bhajan Lal, ex-C.M. Haryana,
DOB: 6.10.1930, 5.40 P.M., Hissar.

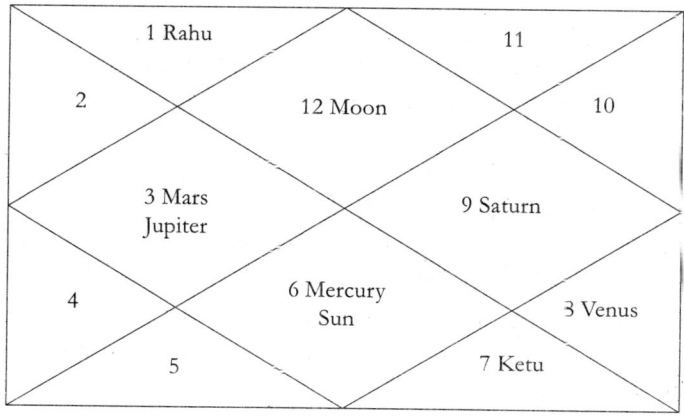

Lagna Moon	Rahu		Mars Jupiter
Saturn	Venus	Ketu	Mercury Sun

Six planets are in four *Kendras* and Venus is in 9th house. Mercury is exalted in 7th house. He is famous as a shrewd leader and was Chief Minister of Haryana for a long spell. He is one of the richest persons of the State.

Jupiter is also *Lagna* and *Rasi* lord, and posited in 4th *Kendra*. He was at his peak during middle age.

4. *Karka* Planets

Acharya Varahamihir has mentioned the requirement for becoming *Karka* planet as follows:

स्वर्क्ष तुङ्ग मूलत्रिकोणगाः कण्टकेषु यावन्त आश्रिताः।
सर्व एव तेऽन्योन्यकारकाः कर्मगस्तु तेषां विशेषतः॥

(*Brihat Jatak*, XXII, Sl.1)

meaning, "Planets in *Kendras* when they happen to be in their own, exaltation or *Mooltrikona* sign become mutually *Karka*. Of these, the planet in the 10th will be best *Karka*."

He gives the example of *Karka* planets in the next *Sloka* stating, "If birth falls in Cancer with Moon in it, and Mars, Saturn, Sun and Jupiter are in exaltation, they become mutual *Karkas*."

Example Chart

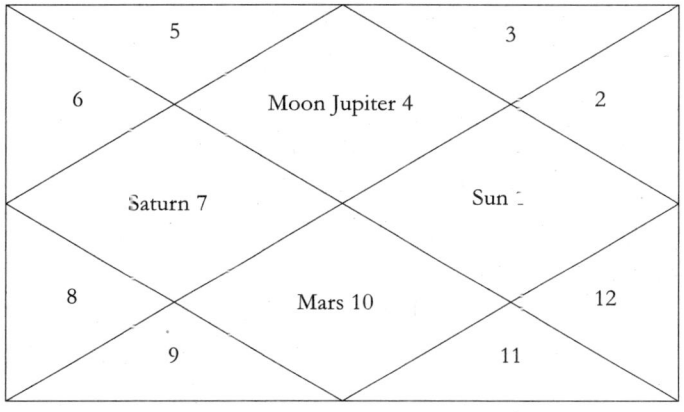

In the example chart the Sun being in 10th from Moon and Jupiter, becomes the most powerful *Karka*.

Karka planets become mutually supportive, even though these be inherently inimical, such as Saturn-Mars, or Saturn–Sun. For becoming *Karka* there should be minimum two planets in *Kendra* in own, *Mooltrikona* or exaltation sign.

Highlighting the importance of *Karka* planets in a horoscope *Saravali* states:

नीचकुले संभूत: कारक विहगै प्रधानता याति।
क्षितिपतिवंश समुत्थो भवति नरेन्द्र न सन्देह:॥

(Ch. VI.5)

meaning, "Even though a person may be born in low family, he will become Chief if there are *Karka* planets in the horoscope. One born in royal family undoubtedly becomes King."

(1) Shri M. Karunanidhi, C.M. Tamilnadu,
    DOB: 3.6.1924, 9.40 A.M., Tirikuvlai (T.N.).

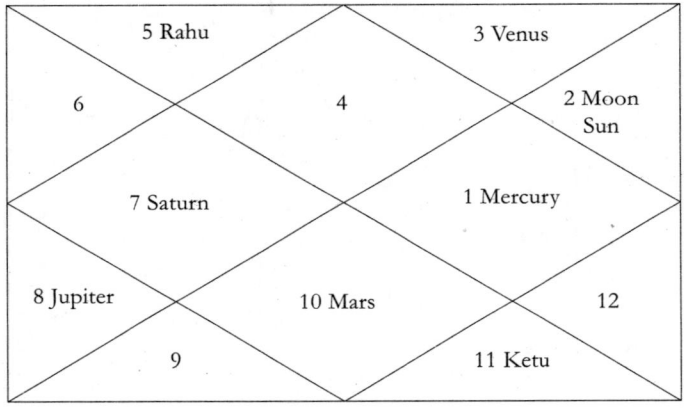

Lucky Births

Saturn is exalted in 4th *Kendra*, and Mars is exalted in 7th *Kendra*. Both achieve the status of *Karka* planets. Saturn forms *Sasa Yoga* and Mars forms *Ruchuk Yoga*. There is *Gajakesari Yoga*, and 9th lord Jupiter aspects *Lagna* and *Lagna* lord. Saturn and Mars also aspect *Lagna* making it very strong. He was earlier also Chief Minister of Tamilnadu and Cabinet Minister at the Centre.

The foregoing discussion makes it clear that the natives having benefic planetary combinations for lucky birth in their horoscopes enjoy the best of this world in their life.

Chapter XIII
Horoscopic Evaluation at First Glance

Every individual born in this world has his unique physical, mental and success pattern. Some youth mature and blossom early, while others do not until quite late. Sometimes child prodigies fail to fulfil their early promise, while average students make their mark in life and become world famous like Sir Winston Churchill and Bill Gates. With the help of some fundamental rules of Astrology one can broadly judge the personality traits and life pattern of an individual by looking at his horoscope for a short while, leaving specific details for comprehensive study. On knowing his potential and future prospects an individual can work upon his capabilities and achieve maximum success in life.

Birth Time

The best time for birth is from 11 A.M. to 12.30 P.M. when the Sun, Mercury and Venus are near about the 10th house (Zenith) and disposed to give the best result.

Children born in the early morning hour are generally more fortunate than those born near sunset. Sunrise is particularly favourable for male children. The Sun occupying *Lagna* at birth infuses ambition and makes them enterprising. Sunrise children are usually their own masters. They love to shoulder greater responsibility and detest a subordinate or inferior position. The presence of other benefic planetary *Yogas* in the horoscope and their *Dasa* during active years of life helps in prosperity.

Some Basic Rules

(1) When the *Lagna* lord is in *Lagna*, *Kendra*, *Trikona* or 11th house, and the *Lagna* and its lord are aspected by benefics, without any

malefic influence, the native even if born in an ordinary family makes his mark in life.

(2) When Jupiter, Venus and Mercury are in *Kendra* or *Trikona*, the native becomes learned, wealthy and famous.

(3) When two or more planets are in own, *Mooltrikona*, exaltation or *Vargottam* sign, and posited in benefic house (other than 6th, 8th or 12th), the native becomes successful and prosperous in life.

(4) Benefics (other than Moon) on either or both sides of the Sun makes the native self reliant and he attains prosperity in life by his own merit.

(5) Benefics (other than Sun) on either or both sides of the Moon with *Pakshabala* (strong in bright fortnight) make the individual mentally strong, successful, happy and prosperous in life.

(6) When the 9th house (luck) is occupied by its lord or benefics, or aspected by these, the native is lucky and prospers in life.

(7) The mutual aspect of *Kendra* and *Trikona* lords, or their exchange of houses or conjunction in a benefic house, makes the native successful and prosperous in life.

(8) Benefics in *Kendras* and malefics in 3rd, 6th and 11th houses ensure a successful and prosperous life.

(9) The 6th, 8th and 12th houses vacant indicates a life free from major troubles in life. The lords of these houses in these very houses in any order form *Vipreet Raj Yoga* and give prosperity in their *Dasa*.

(10) Malefics in *Kendras*, 2nd and 9th houses make the native poor and he struggles in life.

Strong *Lagna*

The *Rasi* (sign) of Zodiac rising on the Eastern horizon at the time, date and place of birth is called *Lagna*. It indicates in brief the health, personality, status, wealth and success in life. *Lagna* lord (whether benefic or malefic) posited in *Lagna* or aspecting *Lagna* gives good result. When *Lagna* belongs to a benefic planet and is also associated with its lord or other benefics, the native gets comforts in life from early childhood. This is not so if the *Lagna* is associated with malefics (*Sarvartha Chintamani*, II.94). This is amply demonstrated in the following horoscope.

(1) Male, DOB: 14.6.1967, 8.45 A.M., Calcutta.

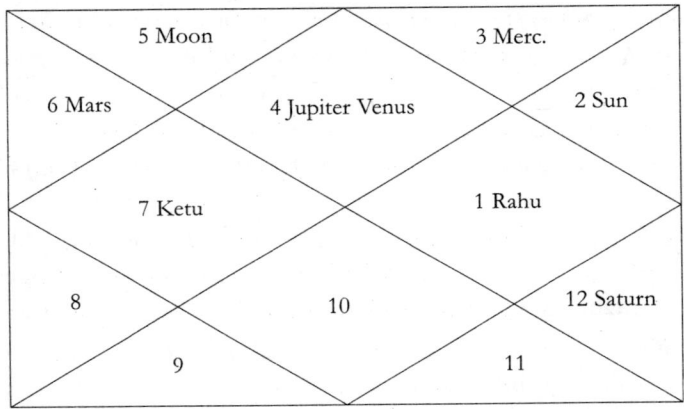

This is the horoscope of a leading industrialist of India. The *Lagna* falls in benefic Cancer sign, with benefics on both sides forming *Shubhkartari Yoga*. Exalted 9th lord Jupiter in *Lagna* forms *Hamsa Panch Mahapurusha Yoga*, and aspects 9th house. The conjunction of the 9th lord Jupiter and 4th lord Venus in *Lagna* shows lucky birth and luxurious life. The *Lagna* lord Moon is in 2nd house, the 2nd lord Sun is in the 11th house, and the 11th lord Venus is in *Lagna* with 9th lord Jupiter. These form excellent *Dhana Yogas*. Six planets are placed from the 11th to the 3rd house thereby forming *Vijeya Malika Yoga*. *Yoga karka* Mars aspects the 9th house and its own sign in 10th house. The horoscope thus not only shows a lucky birth but also a progressive and prosperous life.

(2) Male, DOB: 6.9.1924, 11.46 A.M., Dera Ismail Khan, (Pakistan).

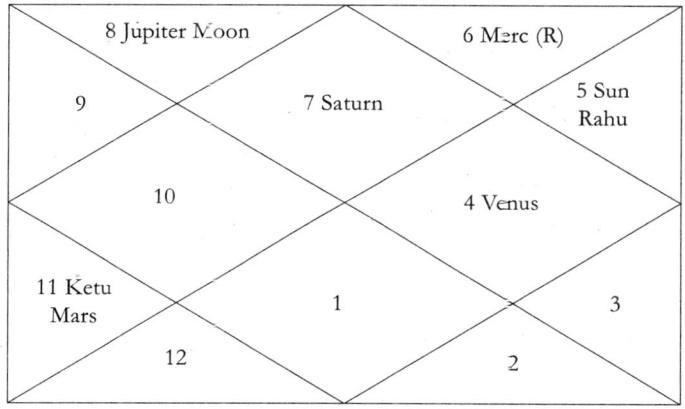

The *Lagna* falls in benefic sign Libra. It is in *Shubhakartari Yoga*, and occupied by exalted *Yoga karka* Saturn forming *Sas Panch Mahapurusha Yoga*. *Lagna* lord Venus in 10th house forms *Amla Yoga*. It is aspected by exalted Saturn and Jupiter. The 9th lord Mercury exalted in 12th house confers religious inclination. The 10th lord Moon with Jupiter forms *Gajakesari Yoga*. The 11th lord Sun in 11th house during birth, away from Rahu, confers name and fame. The strong *Lagna* and *Lagna* lord coupled with other benefic *Yogas* has blessed the native with long life and made him world famous astrologer.

When the *Lagna* lord occupies a *Kendra* (angle) or *Trikona* (trine) with clear rays (not combust by the Sun) in exaltation or friendly sign, lord of 8th house is located elsewhere than a *Kendra*, and the *Lagna* is occupied by a benefic, the native will be blessed with a long life and wealth. He will be handsome, pious, endowed with good qualities, recognized by the ruler and fortunate (*Phaladeepika*, XVI.2). These features are present in the horoscope of Gurudev Rabindranath Tagore discussed below.

(3) DOB: 07.05.1861, 02.51 A.M., Calcutta.

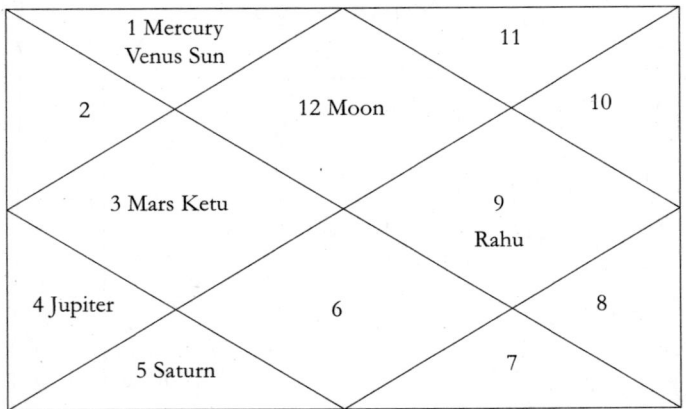

Lagna Moon	Sun Mercury Venus		Mars Ketu
			Jupiter
			Saturn
Rahu			

Benefic sign Pisces rises in *Lagna* owned by Jupiter, who is exalted in 5th house, and aspects *Lagna*. The 5th lord Moon is in *Lagna* (exchange of houses) which made Tagore noble, learned and talented. Exalted Sun and Mercury in 2nd house form a powerful *Budha-Aditya Yoga*, and conjunction of Venus made him a world famous poet and artist. He was conferred Nobel Prize for Literature.

In contrast see the following horoscope.

(4) DOB: 18.07.1962, 10.30 A.M., Delhi.

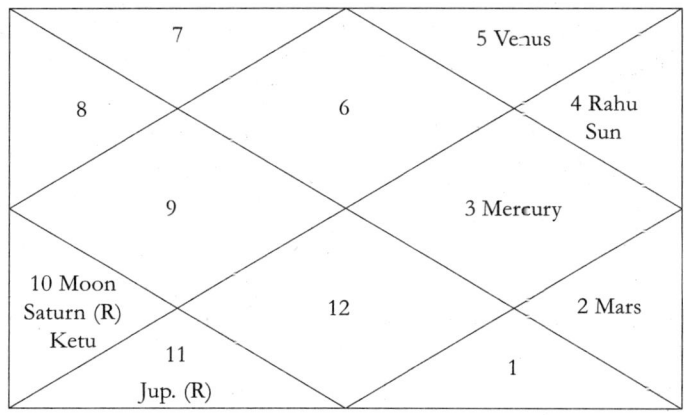

		Mars	Mercury
Jupiter (R)			Rahu Sun
Saturn (R) Moon Ketu			Venus
			Lagna

Virgo *Lagna* rises, whose lord Mercury is in 10th house in own sign which shows high status of his father and comfortable childhood. There is no benefic aspect on *Lagna*, and *Lagna* lord is in *Pap kartari Yoga* which restricted his progress. Jupiter is retrograde in 6th house. Venus, lord of 2nd and 9th houses, is in the 12th house in inimical sign and *Pap kartari Yoga*. It is aspected by malefic Mars and retrograde Jupiter from 6th. The lord of 5th Saturn is retrograde in 5th house with Moon and Ketu aspected by Rahu and the Sun from 11th house. Thus, the *Lagna* lord Mercury, Jupiter, Moon, and lords of 2nd, 4th, 5th and 9th houses are all afflicted. The native, son of a Chief Engineer, could not pass his Secondary School Examination even after vigorous coaching and many attempts. He is working as a salesman in a firm.

Indications for Early Success

Individuals born with Airy signs (Gemini, Libra, Aquarius) in *Lagna* have sharp intellect, good power of expression, and appealing personality due to the influence of favourable Mercury. Gemini born have sharp intellect and they quickly assimilate new ideas and knowledge. Librans are known for their artistry and pleasing manners, while Aquarians have originality of ideas and creativity. Persons born in these three *Lagnas* get an early break in life.

(5) Male, DOB: 8.8.1912, 19.12 hrs, Bangalore.

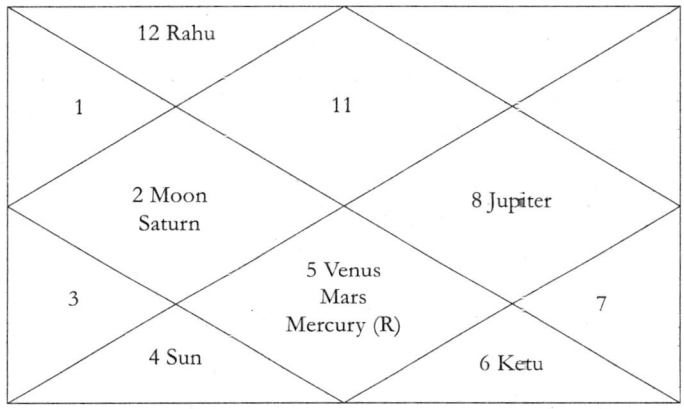

This is the horoscope of Dr. B.V. Raman, famous astrologer. *Lagna* lord Saturn is in friendly sign in *Kendra* (4th house) conjoined with exalted Moon, and aspects *Lagna*. *Lagna* gets *Kendra* effect from benefic Jupiter. There is conjunction of 5th, 9th, and 10th lords in 7th house, and these aspect *Lagna*. Six planets including benefic Jupiter, Moon, Venus and Mercury, are in *Kendra* which is rare and give remarkable achievements in life. The exalted Moon in the 4th house with *Lagna* lord Saturn made him very noble and gentle, and blessed him with excellent memory, mathematical acumen and foresight. Moon also forms *Gajakesari Yoga* with Jupiter in *Kendra* from it, which ensures success and fame in life. Jupiter in 10th house in a friendly sign, aspected by exalted Moon and *Lagna* lord Saturn indicates pious and research oriented profession. He re-started the publication of the *Astrological Magazine* at the age of 24 years and wrote many informative books on astrology. He became world famous by foretelling many important national and international events. He had a long life of over ninety years.

Normal Development

Individuals born under Aries, Leo and Scorpio *Lagna* follow the normal pattern. Due to the influence of Sun and Mars, they are vigorous and fired with ambition for worldly achievements in their 20's and 30's. During this period they show tremendous drive, great force of personality and marked talent for organizational and administrative matters. Most of the whiz kids of modern commerce and industry are born under these signs. The 20's and 30's are the high water-mark of their life.

(6) Male, DOB: 3.12.1965, 6.55 A.M., Agra (U.P.).

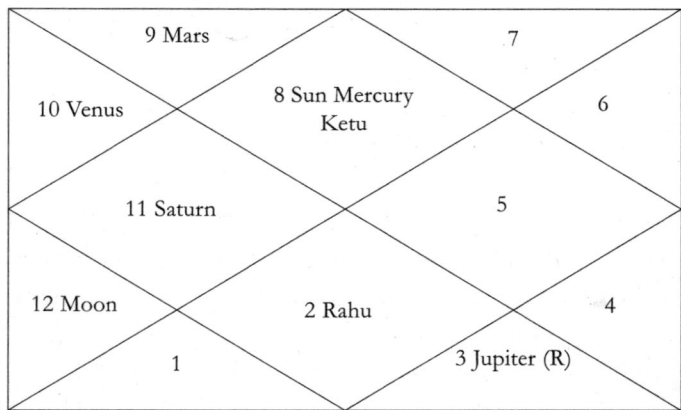

Moon		Rahu	Jup. (R)
Saturn			
Venus			
Mars	*Lagna* Sun Mercury Ketu		

The Sun, lord of 10th house, is in a friendly sign in *Lagna* with 11th lord Mercury forming *Buddha-Aditya Yoga*. *Lagna* lord Mars in 2nd is aspected by 2nd and 5th lord Jupiter. *Lagna* is also aspected by Saturn, forming *Sasa Panch Mahapurusha Yoga* in 4th house, and exalted Rahu in 7th. There is *Shubh Graha Malika Yoga* from *Lagna* to 5th house.

The native after completing B. Com (Hons.) and M.B.A., started with a job of Rs. 10,000/- p.m., changed the Company after a year, and then got an opening in a Hong Kong based garment Export House. He served at Manila, Colombo, Dubai and Dhaka, and through his hard work and enterprise he became Vice-President of the company and was drawing US $2,500.00 p.m. with free residence and conveyance. He unfortunately died with three others in a car accident at Dhaka on July 5, 1993 in *Dasa-Chidra* of Mercury-Saturn.

Middle Age Blossoming

The 40's are the settling down time for Taurus, Cancer and Sagittarius *Lagna* born individuals. Prior to that they remain busy in overcoming various hurdles in life. After establishing themselves in career/profession, and with decrease of their responsibilities, they enjoy comfortable and satisfying life. In this connection the horoscope of our first P.M. Pt. Jawahar Lal Nehru is discussed below.

(7) DOB: 14.11.1889, 23.13 hrs., Allahabad.

		Rahu	
		Lagna Moon	
		Saturn	
Jupiter Ketu	Sun	Venus Mercury	Mars

Benefic sign Cancer rises in *Lagna*. It is in *Pap kartari Yoga*, without any other malefic aspect. The *Lagna* lord Moon is in *Lagna* with *Pakshabala* and seven planets from 1st to 6th houses form an excellent *Graha Malika Yoga* giving strength to *Lagna*. Venus in own sign in *Kendra* forms *Malavya Panch Mahapurusha Yoga*. The 9th lord Jupiter is aspected by *Yoga karka* and 10th lord Mars. Jupiter, Mars, Venus and Mercury aspect the 10th house which indicates great achievements in life. Nehru Ji remained away from home for studies in U.K. On return to India he plunged himself into the Independence Movement and went to jail many times. He became President of Congress Party in 1929 at the Lahore Session and raised the demand of *Poorna Swaraj* under the guidance of Mahatma Gandhi. He was the chief negotiator of Indian National Congress, and Head of Interim Government. India on gaining independence on 15th August, 1947, he was unanimously elected as the first Prime Minister of India and held that post till his death.

Slow Starters and Good Finishers

Natives born in Capricorn *Lagna*, the negative sign of Saturn, have a reserved nature, lack confidence and have difficulty in self-expression during early life. The same holds good in respect of those born in other *Lagnas* in whose horoscope Saturn is close to the *Lagna*. It is not until the age of 36 that their personality begins to mature and blossom. Their physical and mental vitality increases with age. Capricorn natives usually lead a vigorous and active life long after their contemporaries have opted for retirement.

(8) Female, DOB: 31.3.1961, 3.10 A.M., Agra (U.P.).

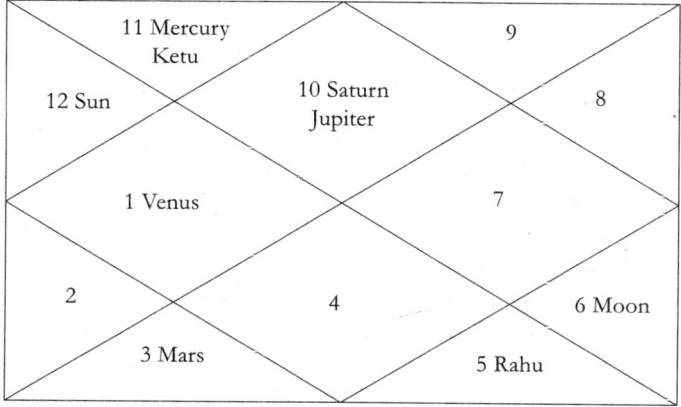

Sun	Venus		Mars
Mercury Ketu			
Lagna Saturn Jupiter			Rahu
			Moon

The *Lagna* is Capricorn which is occupied by its lord Saturn and debilitated 3rd and 12th lord Jupiter, which gets *Neecha Bhanga*. *Lagna* is aspected by 4th and 11th lord Mars posited in 6th house. The native had to look after her ailing mother during her educational years which had adverse effect, but with determination she completed M.A. (English) and B.Ed. Again due to illness of her mother-in-law she had to leave her teaching assignments many times. The native still looked forward to make the best use of her academic qualifications.

Old age also brings contentment and tranquillity to Virgo and Pisces *Lagna* born. These natives have a variegated career, with frequent ups and downs of fortune and face unhappy emotional experiences in love. They are gifted with creative and artistic ability, however, very often they lack practicality. They are too idealistic and theorist in their approach to life and people. It is not until they have learnt through tough experience that their real potential becomes manifest. These natives tend to be episodic, that is, they can at any time flash into brilliance and achieve success, only to recede back into their shell. It is in their later life that they tend to achieve lasting prestige and recognition, which was denied to them earlier due to their inconsistency. There is often a lack of worldliness in Virgo and Pisces natives, which is found in abundance in Aries, Leo and Scorpio born natives.

Progressive Period of Life

(1) If strong planets (in own or exaltation sign) are in the first half of the horoscope (from the 1st to 6th houses these boost the native's luck in the first half of life. But if such planets are located in the 2nd half of the horoscope (from 7th to 12th houses) these give good result in the second half of life. In case such planets are scattered in both halves, one enjoys luck evenly depending on the strength of planets. (*Sarvartha Chintamani*, IX.16)

(2) If Venus is in the *Lagna*, the native is happy in the first half of his life. When there are malefics in the 4th and 5th houses, he gets troubles in the latter half of life. (*ibid*, II.105)

(3) If Jupiter, *Lagna* lord and Moon *Rasi* lord occupy *Kendra*, the person will have happiness in middle age. (*Brhat Jataka*, XXII.5)

(4) Another method given in *Sarvartha Chintamani* (IX.17-19) is as follows. In this method the total life span, say 75 years, is divided into three equal parts of 25 years each.

  (i) 1st part (Upto 25 years) covers 12th to 3rd houses, i.e., childhood to youth.

  (ii) 2nd part (26 to 50 years) covers 4th to 7th houses, i.e., middle portion of life.

  (iii) 3rd part (after 50 years) covers 8th to 11th houses, i.e., later life.

When the 1st part (12th to 3rd houses) is occupied by strong natural benefics, these give good result in early life. When the strong benefic planets are in the 2nd or 3rd part, good results are experienced in middle and old age respectively. The section of horoscope which contains malefics and debilitated or eclipsed planets, causes troubles and difficulties to the native in corresponding age period.

Chapter XIV
Epilogue

(Recapitulation) Resume Of Important Rules

Exact date, time and place of birth is indispensable for erecting a detailed computerized horoscope. Success of prediction depends on the accuracy of the horoscope. *Lagna* (1st house) is the pivot of the horoscope, and indicates in brief the individual's personality, temperament, character, status and success in life.

Lagna degree is the mid point of first *Bhava* (house) which extends approximately 15° on either side. Subsequent *Bhavas* are determined by progressively adding 30° to *Bhava* beginning. *Bhava* position of a planet influences its result. The twelve *Bhava seriatim* primarily deal with self/body, wealth/family, brother/efforts, mother/happiness, son/progeny, enemy/injury, spouse/partner, obstacles/longevity, luck/religion, profession/status, gains, and loss. Due to their nature, the 6th, 8th and 12th *Bhava* and their lords are regarded evil, 8th being the worst.

A house without any planet is regarded weak. If it is neither associated with, nor aspected by a planet, the house result depends on the strength of house lord. Location of a benefic or house lord (whether benefic or malefic) in the house or its aspect increases house strength, while location or aspect of malefic is harmful. House effect increases in proportion to the strength of the house lord, *Karka* of the house, and benefic planets occupying or aspecting the house. A house, its lord or *Karka* in *Papa Madhya* (malefics on both sides) becomes weak. The 8th house from *Lagna* is the house of longevity, as also 3rd house (8th from 8th). The 12th house from these, i.e., 2nd and 7th house, their lords and planets located therein are considered *Marka* (death inflicting). The 7th lord is greater *Marka* than others. Saturn when associated with a *Marka* planet takes over that role and becomes first rate *Marka*.

Epilogue

Shadvarga Charts are erected on the basis of *Lagna* Chart for deeper analysis of different aspects of human life, and are examined like *Lagna* Chart. *Shadabala* of a planet is also looked up for assessing its potential for producing result.

Lagna is both a *Kendra* and a *Trikona*, hence most benefic. *Lagna* with its lord or benefics or receiving their aspect becomes strong. Strong *Lagna* and *Lagna* lord ensure healthy and happy life. *Lagna* lord improves the house matters where located, and retains its benefic nature even when it rules an evil (6, 8, 12) house. Natural benefics in *Kendra* or *Trikona* from *Lagna* and *Lagna* lord, or aspecting these, elevate the stature of the horoscope and the native enjoys a prosperous life. Malefics in *Lagna*, or conjoined with *Lagna* lord, or aspecting these, cause mental and physical problems to the individual. *Lagna* lord with malefics in *Trika* (6, 8, 12) house deprives physical comforts to the native.

The Sun is the King of our solar system. A strong Sun at birth removes many defects of the horoscope and confers high status, name and fame to the native. But Sun's location in Libra (in debilitation) in the horoscope indicates lack of parental care, and the native suffers from poor health, fluctuating career, inferior comforts from marriage, and hindrance in child birth, commensurate with its closeness to deep debilitation degree. Strong benefic aspect acts as a saving grace.

The strength of Moon lies in its *Pakshabala*. It has maximum strength on full Moon (*Purnima*). *Pakshbali* Moon in *Lagna* aspected by a benefic planet gives wealth during its *Dasa-Bhukti*. Strong benefic planets in *Kendra* from Moon form fortunate *Yogas* like *Gajkesari* and *Amla*. The dispositor of natal Moon located in *Kendra* promotes success, comforts and well being, according to its strength.

Debilitated Moon in *Rasi* or *Navamsa* Chart can reduce the effect of many good *Yogas* present in the horoscope. One born with weak Moon (on *Chaturdasi* or *Amavasya*) suffers from fluctuating fortunes, and faces hurdles in achieving success in life. Moon in 6th or 8th house with malefic planet causes health problems. Moon devoid of *Pakshabala* and posited in Mars ruled signs, especially Scorpio (debilitated), with malefic aspect becomes strong malefic. It is less evil when strong in *Pakshabala*.

Combust Moon causes illness, often serious, which may turn fatal if it is also combust in *Navamsa* and aspected by malefics.

The strength of the Sun and the Moon is not only essential for the fructification of *Yogas* formed by these, but also of other benefic *Yogas* present in the horoscope. Weak disposition of either of these reduces the potential of the horoscope.

Strong *Lagna* lord, the Sun and the Moon indicate a progressive and prosperous life. Benefics on their both sides form many benefic *Yogas*.

Jupiter, Venus, unafflicted Mercury, and *Pakshabali* Moon are natural benefics, and Mars, Saturn, Rahu and Ketu are natural malefics. The Sun is regarded a cruel planet. Strong and well placed planets give good result of their house location and *Karkatwa*. The *Karkatwa* of different house matters is as follows: The Sun – 1st house, Jupiter – 2nd house, Mars – 3rd house, Moon and Mercury – 4th house, Jupiter – 5th house, Saturn and Mars – 6th house, Venus – 7th house, Saturn – 8th house, Sun and Jupiter – 9th house; Sun, Mercury, Jupiter and Saturn – 10th house, Jupiter – 11th house, and Saturn – 12th house.

All planets have full aspect on 7th house. Jupiter has special full aspect on 5th and 9th place from its location; Saturn on 3rd and 10th place, and Mars on 4th and 8th place.

Sign lordship and strength of planets are as follows:

Planets	Sign Ruled	*Mooltrikona* Sign/degree	Exaltation sign and highest degree	Debilitation sign and highest degree
Sun	Leo	Leo – upto 20°	Aries – 10°	Libra – 10°
Moon	Cancer	Taurus – after 3°	Taurus – 3°	Scorpio – 3°
Mercury	Gemini & Virgo	Virgo – 16-20°	Virgo – 15°	Pisces – 15°
Venus	Taurus & Libra	Libra – upto 15°	Pisces – 27°	Virgo – 27°
Mars	Aries & Scorpio	Aries – upto 12°	Capricorn – 28°	Cancer – 28°
Jupiter	Sagittarius & Pisces	Sagittarius – upto 10°	Cancer – 5°	Capricorn – 5°
Saturn	Capricorn & Aquarius	Aquarius – upto 20°	Libra – 20°	Aries – 20°

Note: With difference of opinion, Rahu is exalted in Taurus/Gemini and Debilitated in Scorpio/Sagittarius. Ketu is exalted/debilitated in opposite sign and degree.

Epilogue

A planet in exaltation gives 100% result, in *Mooltrikona* 75%, in own sign 50%, in friendly sign 25%, in inimical/debilitation sign adverse result. But Saturn reduces miseries and sorrows when strong, while a weak Saturn increases these.

Planets associating in one of the 4 recognised ways form *Yoga*. *Yogas* formed by benefics yield good result. The association of a *Kendra*, and a *Trikona* lord forms better *Yoga*, which gives luck and wealth. The *Raj Yoga* formed by 9th and 10th lords without any malefic influence produces the best result and confers wealth, status, name and fame.

Benefics in houses 6th, 7th, 8th from the Moon or *Lagna* give rise to highly beneficient *Chandradhi* and *Lagnadhi Yoga* respectively. Depending on the number and strength of these benefics, one attains high status in life.

Strong benefics (Jupiter, Venus and Mercury) in *Upachaya* (3rd, 6th, 10th, 11th) houses from *Lagna* or Moon form another benevolent *Yoga* called *Vasuman Yoga* which gives easy success and wealth. The result is better from *Lagna* than Moon. The result is commensurate with the strength and number of benefics in these houses.

The location of Jupiter, Venus and Mercury in *Kendra* or *Trikona* makes one lucky, wealthy and famous. Mercury behaves like the company it keeps. Venus lacks directional strength in 10th house and does not give good result when alone there.

The location of Jupiter, Venus, Mercury, Mars and Saturn in their own, *Mooltrikona* or exaltation sign in *Kendra* form famous *Pancha Mahapurusha Yogas* conferring high status to the native.

Among the *Trika* (6th, 8th, 12th) houses, 8th house and its lord are considered the most malefic. Any house lord in a *Trika* house, or a *Trika* lord in any house, spoils that house result. An exalted or own sign planet in *Trika* house does not cause much harm. The lords of *Trika* houses placed in these very houses in any order form *Vipreet Raj Yoga*, which gives success and wealth. But their joint *Dasa-Bhukti* causes health problems. However, it is good to have evil lords in evil houses only, and their dispositors be strongly placed in the horoscope.

All planets continuously occupying four or more houses (like a garland) confer progressively greater success upon the native, provided the chain does not start from 8th or 12th house. For example, a person having all the planets from 1st to 5th houses in his horoscope will be considered lucky.

A planet exalted in *Lagna* Chart becomes highly beneficient if it is also exalted in *Navamsa*.

An exalted planet in 5th or 9th house makes one famous and wealthy. Malefics in 3rd, 6th and 11th houses give wealth.

A planet simultaneously owning a *Kendra* and *Trikona* house becomes *Yoga karka* (very beneficial), even if it be a natural malefic. For example, Saturn becomes *Yoga karka* for Taurus and Libra *Lagna*, and Mars for Cancer and Leo *Lagna*.

Mercury, Venus and Jupiter are progressively more fruitful in benefic *Rasi*. The Sun, Mars, Saturn and Rahu are progressively more malefic in malefic *Rasi*, except in their own or exaltation sign. Benefics are strong in *Shukla Paksha* and day time, while malefics are strong in *Krishna Paksha* and during night. Mercury is always strong. Mercury is particularly strong during morning, the Sun during noon, and Saturn in evening. Jupiter is always strong.

A planet in debilitation or in an inimical sign, if *vargottam* or in a good *Navamsa* or getting *Neecha Bhanga*, loses its weakness and gives good result.

A debilitated or combust planet in *Lagna* Chart when placed in an auspicious *Rasi* in prominent *Varga* (Divisional) Charts (*Drekkana, Chaturthamsa, Navamsa, Dasamsa* and *Dwadasmsa*) gives some favourable result.

A combust planet loses much of the result of the house where posited, but not much of its effect pertaining to its house lordship.

A planet (benefic or malefic) ruling a *Kendra* (4th, 7th, 10th) house becomes neutral. If natural benefic owning *Kendra* also owns 3rd, 6th, or 11th house, it becomes inauspicious, while a malefic planet becomes mediocre. The lord of a *Trikona* (1st, 5th, 9th) house in this situation loses some of its benevolence.

Superior planets (Mars, Jupiter and Saturn) become retrograde when transiting opposite to the Sun. By getting full rays of the Sun (like full Moon) these attain full *Cheshta Bala* (1 *Rupa*) and become more benefic or malefic as the case be. According to Maharishi Parasara, when a planet gets *Ati-Vakri* (in deep retrogression) and is about to enter the previous sign, it loses most of its beneficence. Inferior planets (Mercury and Venus) during retrogression remain between the Sun and earth with their darker side towards earth. As a result their radiation is almost nil and this increases their maleficence in proportion to their location and weakness. Many retrograde planets in birth chart give success after much effort.

The majority view is that a retrograde planet in exaltation does not behave as if in debilitation, while retrograde planet in debilitation does not behave as if exalted. A deeply retrograde and debilitated planet retains its debilitation effect.

Chhayagrahas Rahu and Ketu produce special result. When placed alone in any house these give the result of that house lord. Rahu or Ketu posited in a *Kendra* or *Trikona* in association with a *Trikona* or *Kendra* lord, give very good result like a *Yoga karka*. Rahu conjoined with many planets gives the result of the strongest among these.

Rahu in Aries, Taurus and Cancer *Lagna* protects the native against all troubles, Rahu in houses 3rd, 6th, 11th conjunct with, or aspected by, benefic planet gives good result. Ketu in 5th, 7th and 9th houses does not give good result.

Lagna Nakshatra Lord (LNL) and the lord of the *Nakshatra* occupied by the Moon, strongly placed in an auspicious house give good result. A weak *Lagna Nakshatra* Lord cuts short the good effect of the house it occupies, when it also owns the 8th house.

When malefics occupy the preceding and the succeeding *Nakshatra* from the birth *Nakshatra*, the native is devoid of comforts from parents, or he suffers ill health and disease, which may sometimes cause death when there is no association or aspect of benefic planet in *Lagna*. Transit of malefic planets in a similar manner is quite harmful.

The following planetary position gives positive result:

   The Sun in 6th house,

   Full Moon in 4th house (when not eclipsed),

   Saturn in 3rd house,

   Venus in 1st house (*Lagna*),

   Any planet in 11th house.

Planets in *Digbala* (Directional strength) give good result:

   Jupiter and Mercury - in *Lagna* (East),

   Saturn - in 7th house (West), especially in Libra, Capricorn and Aquarius,

   Venus and Moon - in 4th house (North),

   The Sun and Mars - in 10th house (South).

In following paired planets, the first one of each pair gains in strength and does good:

   Saturn and Sun

   Mars and Saturn

   Jupiter and Mars

   Moon and Jupiter

   Venus and Moon

   Mercury and Venus

   Moon and Mercury

The following planetary location causes trouble and hampers that house effect as per dictum *Karko Bhava Nasaya* (i.e., *Karka* of a house in that very house damages its significations.)

   The Sun in 9th house (father),

   The Moon in 4th house (mother),

   Mars in 3rd house (younger sibling),

   Venus in 7th house (spouse),

   Jupiter in 5th house (child/son).

As sole exception Saturn in 8th house increases longevity.

Epilogue

Jupiter spoils the affairs of the house where posited and improves the house and planet it aspects. On the contrary, Saturn improves the house matters where posited, and spoils the houses and planet it aspects.

Venus in 12th house, as an exception, gives prosperity. But when Venus is located in the *Rasi* or *Navasma* of Saturn (Capricorn and Aquarius) the good effects are reduced.

A planet ruling over two signs which fall in two different category of houses, primarily gives the result of that house which it occupies.

A planet having lordship over two signs, and posited anywhere other than its own sign, mainly disburses the effect of the house where its *Mooltrikona* sign falls.

Planets posited in their own sign in houses 5th, 7th, or 11th produce good result even when their other sign falls in evil (6th, 8th or 12th) house.

Timing of Events

Planets produce their result (good or bad), and of the *Yogas* formed by these, during their *Dasa-Bhukti* in accordance with their lordship, location, strength and aspect received.

Strong and well placed planets show special effect of their *Karkatwa* (signification) at the following age:

Sun	22nd year
Moon	24th year
Mars	28th year
Mercury	32nd year
Jupiter	16th year
Venus	25th year
Saturn	36th year
Rahu	42nd year

Vimshottari Dasa is the most dependable for timing of events. When both the *Dasa - Bhukti* and transit are favourable the result is most beneficial. Towards the end of a *Dasa*, the results being experienced get disturbed. This is called *Dasa - Chidra*

Planets give their transit effect as under:
1. The Sun and Mars   - during first 10° of *Rasi*
2. Jupiter and Venus   - during middle 10° of *Rasi*
3. Moon and Saturn   - during the last 10° of *Rasi*
4. Mercury, Rahu/Ketu - during transit of whole *Rasi*

The effect of a *Dasa* lord is significant when a direct planet in natal chart becomes retrograde in transit, and when a planet retrograde in natal chart moves direct in transit. But when a planet retrograde in birth chart during its *Dasa* turns retrograde in transit, it becomes overactive and gives mediocre result.

The *Dasa* of a planet on the last degree of a *Rasi* gives illness, troubles and suffering according to its maleficence.

A benefic planet primarily disburses result of its house placement during first one-third of its *Dasa* period, of its *Rasi* location during the second one-third of *Dasa*, and of aspects on it in the last one-third of the *Dasa*.

A malefic planet gives the result of its *Rasi* placement during the first one-third period of *Dasa*, of house placement in the second one – third of *Dasa* period, and of aspects on it in the last one – third of its *Dasa*.

The *Bhukti* lord friendly to the *Dasa* lord as well as the *Lagna* lord, gives good result during its *Bhukti*.

The *Bhukti* lord enhances the effect of the same house from *Lagna* as it is itself placed from *Dasa* lord.

The *Bhukti* lord in *Kendra*, *Trikona* or *Upachaya* house from the *Dasa* lord gives good result. Its location in houses 6th, 8th or 12th from *Dasa* lord causes troubles and sorrow.

The favourable/unfavourable transit of *Dasa* and *Bhukti* lord, as also other major planets from *Lagna* and natal Moon, influences the final result.

The mutual *Dasa-Bhukti* of Saturn and Venus generally reshuffles the native's life. Similarly, the mutual *Dasa-Bhukti* of Venus and Jupiter causes trouble from family members.

Mutual *Dasa-Bhukti* of Saturn and the Sun ensures success when both of these are strong in their *Rasi* location. When either of these is adversely placed, the period gives distress and grief.

Mutual *Dasa-Bhukti* of weak Jupiter and Mars gives trouble from wife and children.

Mutual *Dasa-Bhukti* of Rahu and Ketu causes trouble, anxiety, accident and disease. The *Dasa-Bhukti* of two malefics is always problematic.

The end of an evil planet's *Dasa* and the beginning of another evil planet *Dasa* (e.g., Rahu *Dasa* after that of Mars) is quite problematic and may cause death in family.

Saturn's transit in 12th, 1st and 2nd to Moon is called *Sade-sati*, and in 4th and 8th to Moon is called *Dhaiya*. People are generally afraid of these transits. But Saturn is *Yoga karka* for Taurus, and Libra *Lagna*, and benefic as *Lagna* lord for Capricorn and Aquarius *Lagna*. It also gives good result for Sagittarius and Pisces *Lagna* born. Saturn does not give much problem in these *Lagnas* during *Sade-sati* and *Dhaiya*, unless Moon is weak and afflicted, and so is Saturn in birth chart.

A house result fructifies when (i) Jupiter, (ii) *Lagna* lord, (iii) House lord, or (iv) the *Karka* of the house transits:

1. The house under consideration,
2. The *Rasi* occupied by the house lord,
3. The *Navamsa Rasi* occupied by the house lord, or
4. Trines (1, 5, 9) from the above *Rasi*.

One should always keep in mind the *Yogas* for Lucky Birth described by Acharya Varahamihir in *Brihat Jatak*:

शुभं वर्गोत्तमे जन्म वेशिस्थाने च सद्ग्रहे।
अशून्येषु च केन्द्रेषु कारकाख्य ग्रहेषु च॥

(Ch. 22, sl. 4)

meaning, "An individual is born lucky if:

1. Birth is in *Vargottam Lagna*,
2. Benefic planets are in 2nd to the Sun (*Vesi Yoga*)

3. *Kendras* are not vacant, and
4. There are *Karak* planets in the horoscope.

Explaining *Karak* planets, he says: "Planets in *Kendras* when these happen to be in their own, in exaltation or in *Mooltrikona* sign, become mutually *Karak* (helpful). Of these the planets in the 10th will be best *Karak*." Such a person born in poor family attains high status in life.

Acharya Varahamihir adds:

मध्ये वयस: सुखप्रदा: केन्द्रस्था गुरूजन्मलग्नपा:।

(ibid, Ch. 22.5)

meaning, "In a horoscope when Jupiter, Moon sign lord, and *Lagna* lord – all the three – are in *Kendra*, then the native enjoys happiness in middle age."

The astrological treatists also mention:

(1) Benefics in 3rd, 6th and 11th houses give good result in childhood. Malefics here give good result in old age.

(2) Benefics in *Lagna*, 4th, 8th, 9th, 10th and 11th houses give good result throughout life. Malefics in these houses make whole life problematic.

Remedial Measures

As regards remedial measures, Maharishi Parasara tells in *Brihat Parasara Hora Sastra* (Ch. 66, Sl.26):

यस्य यश्च दु:स्थ: स तं यत्नेन पूज्येत्।
एषां धात्रा वरोदत्त: 'पूजिता: पूजमिष्यथ'॥

meaning, "At the time when any planet is turning inauspicious for the native, the said planet be propitiated with proper worship (*Puja, Mantra Jap* and *Havan*) and *Daan* (of that planet's things to suitable person), because *Lord Brahama* has given boon to planets that whoever would worship them, they (the planets) would do good to him."

The evil effect of a planet can be reduced to make events bearable, but it cannot be removed altogether.